Yes Mommy

The Mayhem and Madness of Not Saying No

Amy Sprenger

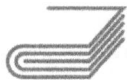

Sheffield Publishing Group

For Jackson, Emily and Maeven, there definitely won't be a "Yes Mommy" when you're teenagers, so I hope you enjoyed it while it lasted.

PROLOGUE

"Stop. Please don't do that. I said stop. Aren't you listening, I said no!"

As the parent of a seven-, five- and three-year-old I'm pretty sure I utter those words hundreds of times a day. Some days, thousands. Like today, a day that started like any other day at my house. While stopping my three-year-old from drawing on the hardwood floors with a Sharpie, I had to explain to the five-year-old that sundresses are for summer and not eighteen-degree Chicago days as I tried valiantly (and unsuccessfully, I might add) to stop the seven-year-old from walloping the five-year-old fashionista during a fight over the Wii controller. I'm living the dream!

And it's not just everyday life either – I recently administered a timeout at Disneyworld after all three children fought over, and ultimately ripped to shreds, a free park map. The sad part is, they all *had their own maps*, they just wanted the same one at the same time. My kids couldn't even keep it together at the most magical place on earth.

Maybe it's me. Perhaps I'm too uptight and I just need to relax and be the mom who lets it all roll off her back. The cool mom who lets them finger paint on the dining room walls and grind Play Doh into the living room rug without fighting off a panic attack that the blue Play Doh is mixing with the red Play Doh. The laid-back mom who lets them play Angry Birds on *her* iPad without giving in to the compulsive desire to wipe their sticky fingerprints off the screen every fifteen seconds. But come on, those moms are urban myths. No one really acts like that with her own kids. No, the parents I know all helicopter the hell out of their kids, micromanaging their every move so they can be sure their special snowflakes stay on the straight and narrow. And yes, I am guilty as well.

When my son, Jack, gets the look on his face that he's about to do something premeditatedly wrong, my mothering spidey-sense kicks in to high gear. I can usually spot whatever it is a mile away, and it starts.

1

"Don't even think about it," I say, looking at a large, twisted tree branch on the grassy strip between the sidewalk and the street on our way to school one morning.

"What?" he replies, his eyes never leaving the branch, clearly fashioning it into a weapon in his wee mind. It has great potential, all pointed and sharp on one end, as it cracked off during a recent storm.

"I am telling you right now, do not touch that branch," I say firmly, believing this will be the time he actually listens to me.

And with that, he picks the branch up and swings it around wildly, narrowly missing one sister in the stroller and smacking the other sister in the back of the head. I explode, a stream of words tumbling from my mouth that all break down to the same message: I said no. I now have one crying about getting hit in the head and one crying because he just lost his iPod Touch for the rest of the day. I'm pissed because he defied me and because of that, his sister got hurt. Not to mention the fact I'm annoyed he didn't just listen to me in the first place. I guarantee you this same scenario played out minutes later with another family a few minutes behind us on its own walk to school because I chucked the branch back down on the grass as I dragged my screaming children down the street.

But what if I hadn't said no? What if I had just let natural consequences rule? Reflecting on the situation, I probably could have let him pick the branch up and get a look at it. Was there really harm in that? And if he was careless and hit his sister, the end result would have been the same: he would have lost screen time because he hurt someone. Maybe I'm too over-protective, constantly stepping in to try and prevent things from happening. Maybe I should just chill the hell out.

I've read all the parenting books. I know *How to Talk So Kids Will Listen and Listen So Kids Will Talk*, employing *1-2-3 Magic* so we have *Healthy Sleep Habits, Happy Child*(ren) while *NutureShock*ing the hell out of our previous beliefs. I can psychobabble with the best of 'em, but when it comes to putting it into practice, I have less than stellar results. Oh, I always start out with the best of intentions. I declare this, *this*, is the parenting technique I've been searching for. I start off strong, consulting the book like the Bible. But inevitably, the kids rebel against the new flavor of the week and I end up losing my cool and yelling. I blame the technique, when really I should blame myself, and abandon it because it clearly doesn't work. A few weeks later, I find the parenting book of my dreams. This one's going to work for sure! Shampoo, rinse, repeat for the last seven years.

Maybe the answer lies in pulling back a little, letting them figure things out for themselves. I'm sick of yelling, sick of constantly saying, *"No, Don't,* and *Stop."* And I'm putting my money, err, my words, where my mouth is. Wait, does that even make sense? See, I'm so weary from saying no all the time my brain no longer works.

In a bid to see if my strictness is ruining my parenting, I'm going to stop saying no for a month. Thirty days without "no," "stop" and "don't" passing my lips. This might just kill us all. But will this make me a better parent? Will this make my kids better kids? Will it change our relationship with each other? Will they even notice it's happening? And most important, will I have any sort of vocabulary left without my most-used words spilling forth?

Ever notice how saying a word over and over makes it sound all weird and distorted? You focus on the pronunciation and how the mouth makes a weird shape and the way the sounds reverberate off the tongue and teeth. Soon, you don't even notice what you're saying and you're just making guttural noises and trying not to laugh. That about sums up what it's like to talk to children. I don't even realize when I'm saying "no," "don't" or "stop," because I do it so often.

As part of my prep for *Yes Mommy*, I asked my husband to follow me around and keep track of how many times I said the words "no," "don't" or "stop" in a single day. I didn't want him to tell me when he was doing it or be obvious about it in any way. After the kids were in bed one Saturday night, Josh flipped a small, shiny silver item at me. I caught it on the fly in my right hand and studied it with a puzzled look on my face.

"It's a click counter," he said. "I bought it on Amazon. Check your digits."

I saw the number eighty-seven staring me in the face. I said some variation of "no" to my children *eighty-seven* times. On a Saturday. I estimate the number would be twice as much on a school day when we need to be somewhere on time with shoes and coats in place. And it hit me – this needs to change. I don't want my kids remembering me as the no-fun mom who yelled all the time. My urgency for the project ratcheted up even more.

Yes Mommy is the tale of two parents: the Before Mom, uptight and quick to say no, and the After Mom, laid-back and open to anything. Well, not *anything*. I'm not letting them smoke joints or get stylized sunshine tramp-stamp tattoos. But I am going to spend thirty days trying to be a better mom through the power of positivity.

CHAPTER ONE
YOU WANT TO DO WHAT?!

"Stop! We do not talk about penises at the dinner table. If I hear it again, you're both going to timeout in your rooms," I say with exasperation to my seven-year-old son and five-year-old daughter one night.

As they cackle with laughter, my three-year-old daughter joins in the inappropriateness and lustily yells, "Poo-poo gaga!" While it sounds innocuous, this toddler version of potty talk makes the older two snort milk out of their noses and it all begins anew.

"No!" I say loudly from the kitchen where I am tearing raw spinach into plastic Ikea bowls. The giggles subside to muffled snorts behind hands and into the crooks of arms. My oldest, Jackson, opens his mouth and I shoot him the evil eye, causing him to rethink whatever it was he planned to say. I sprinkle a few seasoned croutons on everyone's salad and spoon some sweet Italian dressing out of a jar. I set the bowls down in front of each child and go back to the kitchen to grab some cantaloupe cubes for everyone.

"Hey, Jack, look at me," my middle daughter, Emily, says. I look over and see Emmie standing up on her chair, her back to the table, flowered skirt around her ankles, mooning her brother and sister. All three start laughing like hyenas.

"No!" I yell. "No no no no no. How many times do I have to remind you we do not show our private parts to other people?"

I grab her from her place at the table and send her to her room while the laughter continues. Sadly, this is not the first time this has happened in our house, and even sadder, it's not the first time at the dinner table.

"What are you thinking?" I ask her, as I lead her by the hand to the stairs, not using my inside voice. "That is so inappropriate. You go to your room for five minutes and don't even think about coming down until then."

"Can I still have dessert?" she asks. Can you still have dessert? Seriously, child? Although this time in her room will likely be less of a punishment and more time for her to think of how she can top her last act with an even more outlandish encore.

Later, as I relate the story to my husband, Josh, he shakes his head and laughs.

"It's not funny!" I say, shoving him on the shoulder as we sit side by side on the couch. "No wonder our kids act like this, you're right there with them."

"No, you're right," he says. "It's completely inappropriate. But you know how the parenting experts say you should pick your battles? How some smaller things are better off ignored and they'll go away because you're not giving them the attention they crave? Maybe this is one of those situations."

"Or, she'll just keep doing it and the next time we're out for burritos at Chipotle, she'll moon the entire restaurant," I say. "We need to set limits and boundaries. All those same experts talk about kids craving consistency and needing rules to thrive."

"No one's saying we shouldn't have boundaries," Josh responds. "But sometimes, someone mooning you at the dinner table is just plain funny. You have to relax a little and laugh."

A few days later, I am still mulling our conversation. Am I too strict? Are my expectations out of line? Maybe I need to relax, learn to go with the flow a little more. Perhaps dinner-table mooning isn't that big of a deal. Maybe I need to be like those hippie commune parents who let their kids run around naked outside, because when they're actually showing their butts all the time, they wouldn't get such a laugh out of it. Nudity is natural! Who cares? Except we live in the middle of a highly dense urban area and letting my kids run around naked outside would likely draw the interest of NBC's *To Catch a Predator*, not to mention Child Protective Services. See, this is why I can't just relax, why I insist on micromanaging everything from combing their hair to crossing the street – if it's not done right, someone will die. Well, definitely with the crossing the street, maybe not so much with the combing the hair. But you can never be too careful.

No. Don't. Stop it. The words fall off my tongue so easily as a parent, I don't even notice when I say them anymore. And I know if I don't realize how often I say them, my kids sure as hell don't hear them. When did I become this person? The one who goes to "no" as the default answer? Oh, right, seven years ago when Jack learned to move, and with each subsequent child who joined the household. No to touching the fireplace, pulling the cat's tail and Mommy's hair. No to biting our friends, not taking a nap and throwing pureed peas on the wall. No to getting out of the big-boy bed, writing on the wall with markers and running into the street. No to poking dead rats in the alley with a stick, misbehaving at school and karate-chopping our friends during Tae Kwon Do. And apparently, no to mooning your siblings at the dinner table, although no one has taken that one to heart. I don't want to be that mom. But I have to be that mom. Emmie can't leave the house in the middle of the winter in Chicago wearing a sundress; she'll freeze to death. Jack can't climb a tree at the park because he'll fall and break his neck. Maeve can't get out of the stroller and walk because she'll slow us down. But really, wouldn't they benefit from the natural consequences of their actions? If Emmie chose to wear her pink spaghetti-strap sundress to school in January, she would learn just how cold one could get when the wind whips off Lake Michigan in the eighteen-degree temperatures. Jack falls out of a tree? Bet he won't climb it again; or if he does, he'll be more careful. When Maeve insists on walking all the way to the grocery store and back, sure it will take longer, but she gets some exercise. Or maybe she realizes how good she has it being pushed around all day and jumps back in the stroller. Either way, she gets to practice a little independence. And isn't that what we're ultimately after as parents? I need to trust the lessons I've tried to teach them have worked inside their little brains and they know that the reason I tell them no is to keep them safe. Mostly. Sometimes it's because I just don't want to deal with the hassle of whatever mess it would create. Mother of the Year, right here.

How would things get done if I couldn't say no? How would I get them to behave and listen? I have three kids under the age of seven – without no in my vocabulary, there's not a snowball's chance in hell we're ever leaving the house again. What would I even say to them if I couldn't say "no"? I might not ever speak to them again.

But the more I think about it, the more appealing it becomes. I casually pitch the idea to Josh one night after the kids are in bed.

"What if we never said no to our kids?" I ask him, as he watches a St. Louis Cardinals game on his computer.

"Son of a … That's the second error this inning," he yells, without looking up. "Did you say something?"

"I said, what if we didn't say no to our kids," I respond exasperatedly.

"They would end up on death row in a matter of days," he replies, eyes not leaving the screen. "Except it wouldn't be like those death-row cases where some last-minute DNA evidence comes along proving them innocent. In their case, the DNA evidence would come along and they'd be proven even more guilty."

"Remember when you told me to lighten up a few weeks ago, that I didn't have to be so strict all the time? Maybe this is the answer."

Now I have his attention. "Are you insane? Our kids don't listen as it is, how would you ever get them to do anything? It would be complete anarchy. I think this is the worst idea you've ever had. Worse even than letting Emmie find out that American Girl stores existed."

"Hear me out. Maybe this experiment is the answer we've been looking for. Maybe this will make me a better mom. Maybe it will make them better kids. Maybe it will change the way we relate to each other. Maybe, just maybe, they'll learn about natural consequences and start taking some responsibility for their own actions and behavior."

"Amy, they're seven, five and three. Some of them don't even pronounce 'responsibility' correctly. The entire motivation for everything they do is doing whatever is going to please them at that very moment in time without any consideration for anyone else or any realization of the consequences their actions might have."

"So they're a lot like you?" I sweetly ask.

"That's not funny, but it is pretty accurate. But that's not my point. My point is they're going to turn into insane people who stay up all night, eat candy for breakfast and never take showers. And you'll never have to cook again because they will insist on eating every meal at McDonald's. In fact, they might just leave home entirely and live at McDonald's. They will be like that *Super Size Me* guy who ate nothing but McDonald's for a month, but instead of becoming fat and sick, our kids will become hyper and crazy. You're going to undo all the hard parenting work we've put in during the last seven years!"

"Listen, don't you think we should perhaps give them a little more credit than this? Jack actually asks to take showers every night because he likes to prolong bedtime and Emmie sneaks cherry tomatoes from the fridge when she thinks we're not looking. Sure, Maeve is a little young to know what's going on, but we barely ever tell her no anyway. That kid is spoiled as the baby of the family. And our kids think the only things they serve at McDonald's are pancakes and ice cream cones. They have no idea what a McNugget even is!"

Josh looks at me like I have two heads. "If you do this, I'm moving to Canada," he says gravely. "I'll have no choice."

"What does that even mean?" I ask. "Isn't that what people threaten to do when they don't like the outcome of a presidential election? What does that accomplish in this situation?"

"I don't know, but I do it when I don't like my wife's outlandish parenting techniques. You can't really blame me, it's just my survival instincts kicking in. Don't you realize they will eat us alive?"

"We're not going to *tell* them, silly. We're just going to do it."

"So you're just going to start saying yes to everything and you don't think they're going to *notice*? Hey Mom, can I have candy for lunch? Yes? That's awesome! Can you buy me a pack of cigarettes? No, not the lights, I prefer menthols. Check out this sweet tattoo I'm going to get on my face, it will really accentuate my nose ring perfectly. Great idea, Amy."

I sigh and continue presenting my case. "Look, I'm clearly not going to let them do anything dangerous or life-threatening. If anyone gets too close to a tattoo parlor, you can be damn sure I'm going to stop it. I might buy them cigarettes, but I'm obviously not going to let them inhale." I get a slight smile out of Josh. "But I really want to see if this makes us a different family. I want to see if it makes me a better mom. What we're doing now certainly isn't working, so what's the harm?"

"Damn it!" Josh yells, startling me. He never swears at me.

"What the hell?" I say snottily. "You don't need to yell at me!"

"Oh, no, sorry. Not you. The Cardinals stranded the bases loaded. No, for you, I don't care. Fine. Whatever. I mean, I'll be in Canada. I'll probably be too busy watching curling on TV. But I get to yell 'I told you so,' when they end up hysterical from lack of sleep and sugar-overload and you can't be mad at me."

"Listen, I need your support here. You don't need to be critical when things don't go as planned. And I certainly don't need to hear 'I told you so.' Besides, that's my line. You can't use it."

"Oh you'll have my support, because I can't wait to see how this turns out, but all bets are off when it comes to 'I told you so.' You don't hold the patent on that."

CHAPTER TWO
SUPERHEROES WEAR PINK

"Girls, we need to get in the car right now, please," I say with as much patience as I can muster, which is about nil by this point of the morning. Emmie and Maeve spent the last hour playing Barbies in the basement, which was actually a freak of nature all on its own. Nobody pulled hair (human or doll), hit or mistreated anyone else. Ballet Teacher Barbie was a little bossy to Ballerina Student Barbie, but that's to be expected.

"Girls, if you come right now, we can get the treats," I say, which elicits the response I expected. I hear little footsteps thundering up the stairs and squeals of delight that there will be snacks involved. I love that my kids think Costco free samples are special treats. Who am I kidding? I think Costco free samples are special treats! Tiny slices of pizza, mini bagel dogs, a pita chip pre-slathered with hummus, a tiny paper thimble of chicken noodle soup, a Dixie cup of orange juice – it's practically a balanced meal as you work your way around the store. You can eat lunch as you pick up fifty-seven rolls of paper towels and a birthday cake for seventy. I once mentioned my love of Costco samples on Twitter and within a day, a *New York Times* reporter contacted me, asking if he could feature me in a story about people cutting costs in the recession and creating meals out of free samples. I hesitated for a minute, because come on, it's the paper of record, but in the end, declined as it made me look desperate, when really, I'm just unable to say no to a piping hot egg roll fresh out of the toaster oven.

Emmie and Maeve appear before me in skorts, tank-tops and Supergirl capes. Pink, shiny, polyester Supergirl capes they "won" at a local street festival. They "won" them by playing the kiddie high-striker game and pounding the hell out of it to ring the bell. They "won" these capes for the low, low price of twenty dollars. Each. Their father is a sucker for carnie games. I could have bought four capes on eBay for less. But they were so proud when they put them on that I guess it was worth it.

"Mommy, we are going to be superheroes at Costco!" Emmie excitedly informs me.

"Oh, sweetie, n——" I stop myself, realizing what I am about to say. It's Day One of the project and I'm still remembering I have to integrate it into our daily routine. "You're sure you want to wear that to Costco? What if it gets dirty?" I am stalling, thinking for a way out of this one. *Why why why do they want to wear capes to Costco? I don't have time for this. It needs to be a quick in-and-out trip for the five-hundred-count garbage bags and the fourteen-pack of diaper wipes. Everyone is going to stare!*

Then I hear my own thoughts and stop myself. What is the big deal? So they wear capes to the store. I once ate lunch at Panera seated next to a fully-costumed, pint-sized Batman. He never even removed his mask to slurp down his tomato soup – thankfully he didn't spill on his uniform as the bat signal suddenly appeared in the sky and he was whisked away by Alfred. And when I say "bat signal" and "Alfred" please know I really mean "dirty diaper" and "his mommy."

"All right, wear them, but if they get ripped, don't come crying to me about it," I say with a tight smile on my face. The girls are ecstatic and Velcro their white flowered sandals faster than I thought possible. Clearly, we should employ superhero capes for school because we'd never argue about putting shoes on ever again. They file out the door and pleasantly climb into their seats. Jack is at camp, so it's just the girls and me this morning and traveling with two is so much easier than three. Kind of a "duh" statement, but you don't realize until you have more children than arms just how luxurious it is to hold all of your charges' hands in a parking lot. It's always the rogue third child holding onto the back of your shirt that you have to worry about sprinting off after a penny on the ground.

We arrive at Costco and despite the promising start to the trip, a battle is brewing over the cart. Costco has the greatest cart setup of the free world: two side-by-side seats up front and a humongous basket in the back. At a svelte thirty-eight pounds, Emmie can still easily fit in the front seat, but she prefers the basket. She likes to face front with her hands gripping the edge of the cart a la Kate Winslet in *Titanic*. Maeve, at thirty pounds, clearly fits the seat-usage criteria, but she deems the seats for babies and refuses to get in. On the rare occasions when I force her into the seat because we're either buying something huge or she is too mischievous to be trusted, she bucks and kicks like a rodeo bull. Last week I allowed her free access to the basket of the cart at Whole Foods and she grabbed a jar of organic marinara sauce from a display, threw it on the ground and laughed maniacally when it smashed into fifty-two pieces – right in front of another mom from school. After that little number, I literally wrestled her into the cart seat while everyone shopping for grass-fed ground beef watched and took notes for their calls to the authorities. So here we are in the midst of the Standoff at the Cart Corral.

"No cart!" Maeve says emphatically.

"I want to ride in the big part!" Emmie yells. One out of two ain't bad, I guess. I grit my teeth. "Fine, Emmie. Maeve, if you don't want to ride in the cart, then you need to hold Mommy's hand the whole time."

"No!" she yells, stamping her sandal for emphasis. Maybe we should have gone with "thirty days of yes" for the children, instead. I take a deep breath as a woman walks by me and laughs. SuperMaeve stamping her foot looks hilarious to everyone but her mother, apparently.

"Listen, if you don't hold my hand, you could get lost. Do you want a stranger to take you?"

SuperEmmie pipes up, "Yeah, Maevie, then you'd never see Mommy again. Ha-ha-ha-ha-haaaaaaa." Someone needs to tell this one the evil laugh belongs to the villain, not the hero in the cape.

SuperMaeve crosses her arms behind her back for emphasis and stands her ground. Exasperated already and we haven't even entered the store, I throw in the towel. "Fine, but you better stay right next to me the whole time if you want the treats." Parenting by bribery is my specialty.

We begin to peruse the aisles, throwing fifty-packs of AAA-batteries and twenty-packs of black dress socks in the cart. SuperMaeve has been following along, getting lots of oohs and ahhs from the white-hair set shopping for their twelve-packs of prune juice. Her pink cape trails along the tile floor, picking up any number of germs and mud balls. But I resolutely ignore the grime, knowing I can burn it, I mean wash it, when we get home. SuperEmmie asks every three seconds when we're going to have a treat and every three seconds I respond, "in a few minutes." We make our way over to the best section of Costco, the alcohol aisle, and I lug a thirty-pack of Bud Light off the shelf and put it next to SuperEmmie in the cart, alongside a couple of bottles of Pinot Noir. SuperEmmie climbs atop the case of beer and sits higher in the cart. Classy.

"Can we please stop buying Mommy drinks and get a snack?" SuperEmmie asks loudly. At least she's polite. I steer the cart toward the packaged refrigerated section and steel myself for the gauntlet. SuperMaeve reaches her tiny hand up for a piece of bread slathered with flavored butter. "Tank you?" she says, still a trace of baby and mixed-up manners in her dialect. The free-sample lady smiles widely and offers her two. "Well, Supergirl, you'll need a full tummy to save the world." SuperMaeve says, "Welcome," and crams both pieces in her mouth at once. The lady hands SuperEmmie two pieces and we've achieved the portion of the trip where total silence takes over. For all of forty-five seconds while they chew and swallow. Then the cries of "more" begin.

We navigate through the pizza, egg rolls and chicken nuggets. The girls go wild over the GoGurt sample and spit out the flaxseed cracker I told them they wouldn't like, but they insisted on tasting anyway. SuperEmmie announces she wants to get out of the cart and since SuperMaeve has kept the world safe from villains thus far, I agree. Two superheroes are better than one when it comes to patrolling the universe, obviously. I lift her out and she and SuperMaeve walk ahead of the cart. A woman about my mother's age stops us and smiles down at the girls.

"Thank goodness you're here," she says. "I think there's a bad guy in the paper towel section!"

SuperMaeve clings to my leg and SuperEmmie's eyes are wide with concern. "Really, Mommy?" she asks. Thanks, lady. "No, not really. She was just joking," I say, narrowing my eyes at my fellow customer. "Sometimes grown-ups say things without *thinking*. They don't mean to *scare* little kids, but they *do*." The woman straightens up and walks away. Seriously, lady, what the hell?

We move on down the aisle and a fifty-two-inch plush bear catches SuperEmmie's eye and she's off and running before I can even think about it. She's leaping tall displays in a single bound on her quest to get her hands on the bear. She wrestles it out of the box it shares with fourteen other plush bears and drags it over to the cart. "Can we get this Mommy?" she asks earnestly.

"Oh sweetie, he lives here at Costco with his mommy and his friends," I say, cleverly avoiding the N-word. "He would be so sad if we took him home."

"He would miss his mommy," SuperMaeve says soberly. She then makes a move to grab him – clearly the wrong move at this juncture.

"Noooooooooo!" SuperEmmie screeches. "It's mine, Maeve!"

Technically, he belongs to no one as we haven't actually purchased him. SuperMaeve pulls SuperEmmie's hair and SuperEmmie retaliates by smacking her as hard as she can across the back. Capes are flying and people are moving out of the way, smirking. If anyone says one word, I am going to chuck a thirteen-pack of canned salmon at his head.

"Maeve and Emmie, please, you're going to hurt the bear." I take the bear and put him back in his box-cave with his friends and the girls go insane. SuperMaeve crumples in a little heap on the filthy floor, hysterically crying. SuperEmmie screams, "I want the bear!" and flies at me with little arms flailing. I catch her and deflect her tiny fists, horrified at the turn the outing has taken. Some hipster dude carrying a fifty-pack of toilet paper on his shoulder turns and stares as my children lose their ever-loving minds in the Costco toy section. Listen dude, go home and wipe your ass with your Charmin big-roll and someday, in a few years, when you're no longer all *ironic*, you'll have kids of your own who will ruin your shopping trips and you'll think back to this day and feel bad that you stared at us. In the meantime, the girls are now crying like someone has beaten them.

"Mommy, can we please have the bear?" SuperEmmie sobs, pleading with me while hanging from my left leg. Well, here's where shit starts gettin' real, yo. It takes every ounce of my strength to not utter the word no. Are you kidding me? This bear costs thirty bucks! And it's bigger than both girls combined. We have no use for this bear. Where's he going to sleep? How much porridge is he going to require? He better be potty-trained, I just got the last one out of diapers. I put a tight smile on my face and announce that yes, the bear can come home with us.

The tantrums immediately stop; SuperMaeve stands up and starts clapping and laughing, with the tears still wet in tracks down her pale face, and SuperEmmie pumps her fist in the air and yells, "Yes!" The bear takes his place in the cart and I can barely see where I am pushing the thing because he's blocking all my sightlines. So everyone's happy and the universe is safe from evil, right? Not so fast.

"The bear is mine, right Mommy?" SuperEmmie asks as we turn toward the checkout. "It can sleep with me?"

"He's not Emmie's bear!" SuperMaeve cries loudly in a panicked voice. "He's my bear! He's going to sleep in my bed with me!"

"Maeve, that bear is bigger than you," I reply with a patient smile.

SuperEmmie helpfully pipes up with an evil hiss, "It might eat you if it sleeps in your bed."

"He will not eat me! He's my friend!" Maeve yells, fresh tears springing to her eyes.

I just can't win.

"Mommy, can't we just get two?" Emmie whines.

And that is how it comes to be that I am now pushing not one, but two, gigantic plush bears in the cart.

The girls are running down the aisle, pink capes flapping behind them. People are pointing and aww-ing in their wakes. It's unclear if they're astonished at the two caped wonders running in front of the cart or the twin four-foot-tall bears in the cart. If Josh ever speaks to me again it will be a small miracle.

A woman stops me and says, "They're just too precious for words." I assume she is referring to my daughters, not our new twin bears. "Enjoy it now, they'll be grown and out of the house before you know it." Usually when someone says something like this, I smile and promptly turn around and have to send someone to timeout for trying to shove a LEGO into someone else's ear canal. But today I actually stop and appreciate it. She's right, they'll be asking me to drop them off three blocks from the mall and begging me to find something more fashionable to wear in no time. They won't want thirty-dollar bears, they'll want two-hundred-dollar pairs of jeans. And they will fall over dead if I ever buy them at Costco.

We check out with the bears, the cashier asking if the superheroes saved them from the evil forces. SuperEmmie, always one for being literal at this age, announces, "No, we wanted them and our mommy said yes!" The cashier laughs and replies, "You're lucky to have such a nice mommy. I would have told my kids no." I smirk and tell her she's clearly a much better parent than I am. But after buckling the caped crusaders into their seats, I wonder if that's really true. Does diffusing a public tantrum by giving in make me a bad parent? Or just one who knows when to cut her losses? My real self would have dragged two hysterical kids down the aisle, probably hissing that they were going to timeout the minute we got home. There would have been a scene and most likely it would have ruined the rest of the day. Instead, we went home happy with smiles on our faces. Sixty dollars lighter, but definitely happier.

I wasn't going to miss a chance to annoy Josh with our little purchase, so I positioned both bears in front of the door so he wouldn't be able to pass by without seeing them when he got home from work. I hear the gate open so I run to the kitchen, pretending I am loading the dishwasher, so I have a partial view of the spectacle about to take place. There's some fumbling of keys before Josh finally opens the door, but he doesn't enter. The door stands ajar for a good ten seconds with no sound before he yells, "Canada!" and slams the door shut again. I giggle. Another fifteen seconds pass before it reopens and Josh calmly announces, "I am going to close this door one more time and if I reopen it in thirty seconds and see these bears again, I will in fact be moving to Canada. I swear I will get back in my car and start driving north until I am literally a Canadian."

"I don't think it quite works that way," I shout from the kitchen. "You'd still be an American. And you don't have your passport, so wouldn't you feel like the biggest idiot when you got all the way to the border?"

The door slams shut again. I run to the door and wrestle the bears out of the way. A few seconds later he opens the door with me standing there instead of the bears. I receive the death stare.

"You don't understand!" I sputter. "The girls had a tantrum and I'm not saying 'no' remember?"

"I don't want to hear it," Josh sighs as he strides past me, "Nothing you say can justify this atrocity."

Josh settles down later that night, amazingly agreeing to talk to me again. I thought it might take a day or two, so this is encouraging. He was softened by the sight of the girls setting up a tea party with their bears on the living-room rug, but assures me we will give them up for adoption at the Salvation Army in a few weeks. The bears, not the girls. As I fill him in on the nonsense from the Costco outing, I realize I might have caused the whole thing to begin with. I was the one who put the original bear back in the box and said he needed to stay at the store. Liar liar, pants on fire. I check on a sound-asleep SuperEmmie, who has turned back into her Clark Kent self in her ballerina jammies, and find her dwarfed by that damn bear in her pink-sheeted twin bed. I have to actually turn the light on in Maeve's room to find her in her own bed as the bear is taking up all available space. I find her huddled in the top corner, laying the short way with her legs sticking off the side while the bear is lengthwise and covered with her baby blanket.

In the grand scheme of things, a couple of thirty-dollar bears for two happy superheroes is the best money I ever spent at Costco. Well, except for that one time when I scored a pair of Seven for all Mankind darkwash jeans for seventy-nine dollars. On second thought, that was definitely money better spent.

CHAPTER THREE
SLEEP IS FOR THE WEAK

If there's one thing we've held sacrosanct in this house from the beginning of time, it's sleep. Jack came home from the hospital and slept all the time. It was brilliant! We had this little baby and he ate, opened his eyes for about ten minutes and then fell peacefully back to sleep for several hours. Who said this was going to be hard? That was awesome. He averaged about twenty hours of sleep per day in those first few weeks and we used to dive for the camera on the rare moments he was awake because we needed pictures of his blue eyes actually open. But then something crazy happened – he started waking up more.

"I don't think this is right," Josh said at the time. "I think he might be defective. He was working just fine when we first got him. Now he's awake all the time. Isn't there some sort of baby warranty?"

"It's already past the thirty-day mark and we removed the tags. I don't think the hospital will take him back now," my sleep-deprived self quipped.

"Well, I'm going to write a letter to the manager of that hospital about this little development. When he was there, those nurses swaddled him up like a baby burrito and he slept twenty-three hours a day. They led me to believe it would be like that forever. I think it was false advertising on their parts."

"Writing letters about baby warranties sounds like a productive use of your time," I told him dryly. "There aren't diapers to be changed or babies to be rocked or anything."

"Would they at least give us store credit?"

"I don't think the hospital has the same return policy as Target."

We might have thought our little jokes about sleeping changes were funny after one month, but by the time he turned three months old we really weren't laughing. It was about this time that Jack realized sleeping all the time was for suckers. Stuff was going on! There were places to go and things to do. He had ladies to charm and grandparents who needed to spoil him. But I found my secret weapon: Dr. Weissbluth and his bible-like book, *Healthy Sleep Habits, Happy Child*. Weissbluth's theory is that well-rested kids make for well-rested parents, which makes for a much happier family. Not to mention inadequate sleep can decrease brain function and cause a host of medical issues. I didn't want a stupid kid, so I bought his theory hook, line and pillow. Jack slept on regular schedules with a whole routine. We used white noise machines, black-out shades and temperature controls. And it worked; he eventually became a regular twelve-hour overnight sleeper. The girls each followed suit and I was one of those smug moms who was able to put her child in a crib, shut the door and welcome them out the next morning. We had some hiccups when they moved out of cribs and into regular beds, but after a few weeks of firm and resolute put-backs, we once again had amazing sleepers.

For the most part, our kids are still great sleepers. They go to bed a little later and wake up a little earlier, but I'm talking going to bed at seven-forty-five instead of seven-fifteen each night. Our kids wake up insanely early no matter how late we put them down, so seven-forty-five it is. But once they're asleep, they stay asleep. Nobody wanders into our bed in the middle of the night, nobody cries about monsters, nobody interrupts Mommy when she's watching *Breaking Bad*. It's a beautiful thing.

But lately, we've experienced some pushback when it comes to bedtimes. Maeve goes to bed beautifully, but when one has a doorknob lock on the *outside* of her doorknob, one really has no choice. But Jack and Emmie have taken to prolonging the inevitable as long as possible. They need cold water, they need to go to the bathroom, they need to change into a different pair of pajamas, they need to play with LEGOs in the hall. Last week, Emmie told me she had to tell me something right then so she didn't forget. "What?!" I asked exasperatedly after fifteen minutes of shenanigans. "Umm, I forgot," she said, twirling her blonde hair around her finger. Get back to bed. Now.

Tonight, I have grave apprehensions about the first Yes Mommy bedtime. Oh sure, I talk a good game about being laid-back, but that doesn't mean I'm not screaming *no no no no no* inside my head while I'm letting it all roll off me on the outside. Perhaps a little meditation would be a good addition to this exercise. I could use "yessssss" as my mantra. Or maybe some booze would be better. A good stiff drink might also relax me right up. And it might make the time pass faster while I am mentally willing them to get back in bed.

I tuck everyone in, ask each of them what their favorite part of the day was (Jack: playing Wii; Emmie: going out for ice cream; Maeve: eating sand in the sand box) and what their wish for tomorrow is (Jack: having a fun day; Emmie: having a fun day; Maeve: eating sand in the sandbox) and dim the hall lights to the exact lumen I have calibrated that allows for enough light to balance yells of "it's too dark" and it being too light, enabling them to play with toys in the shadows. I open doors a crack after protests of them being shut and tell everyone to stay in bed. I head downstairs and steel myself for the onslaught.

I see the light pop on upstairs and the bathroom door clicks shut. I stare at my iPad, resolving to keep reading J.K. Rowling's *The Casual Vacancy* as if nothing is going on. I hear some pounding and water running, but the door doesn't open. I am a rock, not moving from my spot on the couch, although my left eyelid is twitching. Five minutes later, I still hear pounding, now accompanied by singing. The twitch has moved from my eye to my leg. Out of the corner of my eye, I see a little blonde head poke over the bannister.

"Mommy, I have to go to the bathroom and Jack is in there," Emmie says.

"Ask him nicely if you can go in," I say, reluctantly putting my iPad down and closing the magnetic lime-green cover.

"Jaaaaaack, I have to pee, let me in," Emmie whines.

"No!" he says.

She screams, "Jack! Let! Me! In!" as loud as she can while banging on the door. I believe residents of the northwest suburbs heard her potty pleading, but her brother is completely ignoring her. She pounds and he laughs. I finally drag myself upstairs to stage some sort of intervention.

"Jackson, open this door right now," I say firmly. "Your sister needs to go to the bathroom."

I reach for the door handle, which is locked. Unfortunately for Jack, we live in a one-hundred-forty-year-old house that predates even the great Chicago fire. That means our floors slope and our doors don't always hang properly, making them tricky to lock. Bad for privacy, great for access to places in which kids want to hide. I lean my shoulder into the door and it opens, much to Jack's surprise. I find him standing at the sink, with the equivalent of a half-bottle's worth of liquid soap bubbling in the bowl. There are bubbles in the sink, on the counter, on the cabinet and on the floor. There are also bubbles on his face, resembling a beard and mustache, and all over the front of his pajamas. I stare at him open-mouthed for a second, and then escort Emmie into the room so she can finally pee.

"Ho ho ho, little girl, I'm Santa Claus!" he booms in a deep voice, the white bubbles obscuring the bottom of his face. Emmie cackles and tries to swipe at his bubble-beard on her way to the toilet.

"What exactly are you doing?" I ask, knowing full well exactly what he's doing.

"Nothing!" he says quickly. "I was washing my hands and the soap accidentally spilled and I was trying to clean it up."

He *accidentally* spilled a half-bottle of foaming Method handsoap in the sink. The kind you actually have to *pump out* of the bottle to get it to foam. Clearly, an accident. Happens to me all the time. I calmly ask him to clean it up and get back in his room. The old me would have screamed "No!" and told him a million different ways to knock it off. The new me is all Zen and cool about it. I have Emmie just scoop a handful of bubbles out of the sink when she washes her hands in the other sink; why waste what we've already got?

After she's done, I bid her goodnight again and go back to my iPad. Is anyone in Rowling's fictional Pagford happy about anything? These people need some therapy. After a few minutes, I hear giggling. After re-reading the same paragraph eight times, I decide to abandon my novel and switch to Facebook. I "like" a picture of someone's new baby and try to figure out why a grade-school friend is posting pictures of herself looking like a washed-up hooker. Sadly, I'll never know because I hide her posts after realizing I have an irrational anger toward this woman (who I don't even actually remember) for clogging my feed with pictures of her bare midriff. Killer body, yes, but her leathery face shows each of her thirty-nine years, and then some. I still hear giggling and try to decide if I need to go up. The problem is solved for me when Jack comes halfway down the stairs.

"Emmie won't go in her own room," he tattles. "She's keeping me awake."

"No, he told me to come in there," she retorts, joining him on the staircase.

"I think both of you are going to be very tired in the morning," I say. "You should probably get to bed." I go back to scrolling through my feed and they sit there dumbfounded. If they're looking for attention, I'm fresh out of it. They climb back up the stairs and I hear doors closing. Wow, that was easy.

Then I hear doors opening. The hallway light goes off and then back on again. I remain seated with my arms and legs in the vehicle at all times. Oh look, a picture of someone's dog lying on a couch! That's something you don't see every day. Jack parades past me carrying a half-full blue Camelback bottle with dinosaurs on it. "I need cold water," he explains. I watch as he dumps the water into the sink and refills it with fresh water from the Pur dispenser in the fridge, adding ice cubes. Who the heck needs ice cubes in the middle of the night at his bedside? He kisses me and says goodnight again and disappears upstairs. Seconds later, the same act is played out with Emmie and a pink flowered Camelback bottle. No wonder this kid needs to get up and pee a million times a night, she's drinking thirty-two ounces of water before she hits the sack.

My mothering spidey-senses alerts me a light switch has been activated in the upstairs lower-right quadrant. I silently climb to the top of the stairs and observe Jack playing quietly with LEGOs. As I stand there in the dark trying to figure out what to do, Emmie almost crashes right into me as she runs out of her room.

"Mommy! You scared me!" she says.

"If you were in your bed where you belong, you wouldn't have been scared," I reply blithely. She slinks back to her room, looking back over her shoulder to see if I'm watching. I ignore the boy and his mad LEGO skills and duck into my room. I can see the entrance to Emmie's bedroom in the reflection of a floor-to-ceiling window in the hall; I watch as she sits down with a book and starts flipping through the pages by the ambient light from Jack's room a few feet away. Doesn't she know that will ruin her eyesight? They're both quiet, but they're not sleeping, so I can't count it as a victory just yet. I flop onto the bed, taking care to mess the taupe microsuede duvet cover as little as possible, and check out my "What's for Dinner" group on Facebook. Damn, everyone else is making something delicious. I slapped some pasta and sauce on a plate with some broccoli and apple slices and called it a night. One of the group members made beer waffles with Welsh rarebit! I am calling bullshit on that as a weekday recipe.

Little voices are whispering and I check the digital clock on the nightstand to my right – eight-fifty-five p.m. My children have been fooling around for more than an hour. I look up from a fascinating thread discussing the pros and cons of iPhones vs. Droids and see Emmie peeking around the doorjamb. I raise my eyebrows at her, but say nothing.

"Umm, Mommy?" she begins.

"Yes?" I reply, not looking directly at her. I remember when they were babies all the sleep books said not to make eye contact in the middle of the night, because it would encourage them to stay awake longer. I think they should have advised this for older children. And come to think of it, why doesn't anyone write a sleep book for school-age kids? It would make millions. Please, someone, just tell me how to get them in their beds and have them stay there and I'll personally make the book a *New York Times* bestseller.

"For my next birthday, I want a princess mermaid cake," she says. Please note: her next birthday is six months away.

"Great. Why don't you think more about how you'd like it to look while you're sleeping?" I respond, not looking up from the iPad. Why would someone post a picture of her kid peeing on the potty on Facebook? I mean, sure, I have taken pictures of my kids peeing on the potty, but I didn't post them on Facebook. I plan to use those for blackmail during the teenage years.

As she walks by Jack's doorway, they begin a conversation. They're not even pretending to be quiet. Suddenly, I hear screaming and shuffling. I walk into the hallway to find Jack smacking Emmie's back as hard as he can, while she kicks him repeatedly. I calmly separate them, ignoring the cries of "he's hurting me" and walk Emmie back to her room. I put her in bed and wordlessly cover her, then tell her this is the last time I will come in there. I pass back by Jack's room and shut the lights off, drawing a yell of protest. "I can't see my puzzle!" he yelps. He's doing a puzzle. At nine o'clock at night. "Good night," I say sweetly, walking down the hall.

I flip back to my reading app on my iPad and immerse myself in the men and women of Pagford once again. This ain't no *Harry Potter*, but damn, I am hooked. The woman can get inside people's heads. I read a few pages and hear whispering. They must have declared a cease-fire. Someday in the future, after raising these two, I will be awarded the Nobel Peace Prize. I am able to get an entire two chapters in without interruption and I decide to take a peek. I look in Emmie's room first and begin to panic – she's not there. I throw back the covers, frantically look under the bed and actually turn on the light to make sure she's not sleeping on the floor or in the closet. Oh my god, someone took her. Someone sneaked in the house and took her. Or even worse, she decided to leave on her own. My five-year-old daughter climbed out the window and dropped two stories down and is now heading for the local toy store to get a Barbie fix.

I lunge the three steps to Jack's door and practically fall over I stop myself so quickly. The two of them are sound asleep, foot to head, in his twin bed. Emmie has her pink fuzzy blanket nestled next to her face and Jack is sleeping with his arms outstretched above his head. I quickly snap a picture and stand gazing at them a little longer than is normal. I reluctantly back out of the room and shut all the lights off in the bathroom and the hall. I text the picture to Josh with the message, "Finally asleep. Together. Only took three hours and two glasses of wine. For me, not them, obviously."

Sure it took a little (a lot) longer than normal. And had I truly checked out and not let it bother me, it would have been fine. But just because I wanted to be chill doesn't mean it actually happened. I didn't say no, I didn't freak out, I didn't yell; but I also wasn't exactly cool about it. My blood pressure was elevated and I was gritting my teeth to keep my mouth shut. Perhaps next time I should hide in the basement until it's over. Or, just leave them with a sitter and grab dinner with friends.

The next morning, Emmie is up with the sun as usual and wakes Jack up with her. They spend the day bickering and by the witching hour of dinner time, she melts down and starts hysterically crying because Maeve gets to choose the video to watch.

"I don't like *The Wiggles*," she says, sobbing so hard I can barely understand her. "It's for babies!"

"I not a baby!" Maeve shrieks from the couch. Yes, yes, we know. You're a big girl, Maeve.

"Yes you are!" Emmie retorts. "Babies watch *The Wiggles*. I want to watch *Yo Gabba Gabba*!" She kicks her legs on the ground for emphasis.

Now both of them are crying. Maeve can't hear *The Wiggles* because Emmie is screaming, Emmie is screaming because she doesn't want to watch *The Wiggles* in the first place. It's a very vicious circle up in here right now. Jack looks up from his iPod Touch and yells, "Could everyone stop screaming? I am trying to concentrate here!"

"Emmie, what's wrong? I think you need to get control of your emotions," I say soothingly, mentally calculating the minutes until bedtime. Too bad for me the number is not small enough.

"I do *not* need to get control," she sobs.

"Why don't you just go upstairs and calm down for a few minutes before dinner? It's not a punishment, I just think it will help."

"I will *not* calm down," she cries, dragging herself up the stairs.

I go in and start shredding the barbecue pork that's been braising in the slow cooker all day, methodically making it smaller and smaller. I dump in more sauce and stir it all together, leaving it to cook a few extra minutes. I slice the wheat buns and microwave some broccoli, and when I'm done, I realize Emmie hasn't come back downstairs. I call her name from the bottom of the stairs, but don't hear a response. I walk into her room and find her asleep under the covers with the lights on. I brush a few strands of blonde hair back from her cheek and she doesn't move. I say her name a few times, nothing. She stirs slightly, then rolls over and faces the wall, her Cabbage Patch baby, Aspen, clutched tightly in her left arm. I turn off the lights and close her door, heading downstairs to give the other two their dinner. I figure she'll turn up in a few minutes.

The few minutes stretch into an hour. Jack and Maeve head upstairs for showers, making a racket that would wake a comatose patient, yet Emmie sleeps on. I put both Maeve and Jack to bed, and Emmie still slumbers. I reason a sundress is kind of like a nightgown, so she doesn't really need pajamas and one missed night of tooth-brushing won't doom her to a life of fillings. I check on her before I head to bed and she's switched to sleeping at the foot of the bed with all the covers thrown off. I pull a sheet over her as best I can and kiss her forehead.

A little face appears at my bedside the next morning, waking me from a sound sleep. "Mommy? Can I have breakfast?" I squint at the bedside clock and see it's five-forty-five a.m.

"Of course, sweetie. You slept right through dinner last night, you must be starving," I say.

"Mommy, I was really tired."

I pour her a bowl of organic Honey Os in the kitchen and wonder if it's worse to have her up until ten o'clock or awake before six in the morning I'm not equipped to think about these kinds of things this early, so I decide both are terrible options.

"You know, I was so tired because I stayed up late fooling around," she says, happily crunching her cereal and slurping her milk.

"Maybe you won't do that anymore," I say, yawning. Wait, did my five-year-old really just grasp the consequences of her actions? I must be dreaming, yet I am quite aware I am not asleep in my warm bed like I should be.

"No, I probably will," she says, smiling and grasping a Honey O between her thumb and forefinger, popping it in her mouth with relish.

At least she's honest.

CHAPTER FOUR
SIX FLAGS OVER INSANITY

One of the awesome things about living in Chicago is its proximity to nature. My kids are growing up in a major metropolitan city with all the benefits it has to offer: museums, parks, the arts, world-class sports teams (well, outside of the Cubs), easy access to public transportation and potholes as far as the eye can see. It's a beautiful thing. But every once in a while they need to breathe some fresh air and look out over a vista that doesn't include concrete and skyscrapers. Enter the genius of a lake house.

Ninety minutes northwest of the city, Josh's family has a lake house. Jack was still in my belly the first summer they bought it and has literally grown up spending weekends at the lake. He's gone from a baby in the shade on the dock to a seven-year-old who tubes behind the speedboat by himself. Emmie and Maeve love nothing more than to run and jump off the end of the pier, climbing out and repeating it again ad nauseum for entire afternoons. When they emerge for dinner, smelling of lake water, dripping wet with blue lips and shivers running down their skinny legs, I smile and throw a towel at them, knowing they will sleep well after all that activity. Growing up in Wisconsin, I know better than to get in the lake before July Fourth, when it finally reaches a temperature not requiring a wetsuit. And even then, I avoid actually getting in the water as much as possible. There's Muskie in these waters and those things can bite your face off.

As we do many times each summer, we are packing up and heading out for the lake house this morning. The kids are itching to get out of the driveway and everyone is on his and her best behavior, excited to swim and see Grandma Martsi and Grandpa Scott. Conveniently, the lake house is close to my own parents' house, so they usually come to visit and the competition over who can spoil them more begins. Jack is yelling that we need to hurry up and Maeve has actually climbed into her own car seat and buckled herself in. Josh and I bicker over who is going to drive and as always, I lose because he pulls the trump card that he has to "work" on the trip up. I don't usually define playing Scrabble on my phone as "working" but then again, I once tried to tell Jack that I was "working" when I was live-tweeting an episode of *The Bachelorette* and he disdainfully told me that watching television was *not* working. The seven-year-old set clearly knows nothing about social media. Twitter is changing the way we communicate, thank you very much, and the world hangs on my snarky tweets about the lucky Bachelorette and her twenty-five idiot suitors.

I end up getting in the driver's seat yet again, bitching the whole time about how I always drive and it's ridiculous. Josh steadfastly ignores me and opens his laptop. The kids are immersed in their various iProducts in the backseat and we're out beyond the northern suburbs in no time. As we approach the exit for Gurnee, Jack happens to look up from his iPad and exclaims, "Hey, look! Six Flags! Can we go?"

Maeve excitedly adds, "Yeah, can we go der? Please, Mommy?"

Emmie yells, "I want to go on the Wizzler!" Actually it's the Whizzer, but that's neither here nor there right now.

Josh cocks his head and looks at me. "Yes, *Mommy*, can we go there?"

Aww shit, it's on. "Yes! Yes we can," I say with fake enthusiasm, resulting in cheers from the children in the car. I quickly maneuver over three lanes to the exit and get in line behind the other million people looking for a roller coaster fix. The kids are chanting "Six Flags" in the back and Josh is smirking in the passenger seat.

We pony up the twenty-two dollars for parking and after slathering everyone with sunscreen, we head for the ticket booth. The cheerful woman behind the glass informs us it will be a cool sixty-three-ninety-nine for the adults and forty-three-ninety-nine for the kids. Josh, no longer smirking, gives me a dirty look. "This is so coming out of your publishing advance," he says.

Ever the businessman, Josh quickly ascertains that for just a few dollars more, we can upgrade to season passes and come back again. "It's practically criminal not to upgrade," I say meekly.

"Let me be clear: we will use these passes sixty times so it ends up costing us one dollar per visit," Josh says. "It will be the Summer of Six Flags. El Verano de Seis Banderas!"

"Once 'Si Mami' month is over, there's no way I'm taking these kids to Seis Banderas ever again," I say.

"Don't worry the next fifty-nine visits will be to Six Flags Canada, when the kids come visit me in my new home," Josh says.

"They don't have a Six Flags Canada," I say authoritatively.

"Excuse me, miss, do they have a Six Flags in Canada?" Josh asks the woman behind the dirty Plexiglass window.

"Why yes, there sure is," she says excitedly, consulting her computer screen. "It's called LaRonde and it's in Montreal."

Josh's eyes light up and he yells, "Road trip!"

"I can see it now, the Canadian Six Flags features a ride called Yukon Adventure where patrons run from actual grizzly bears," I say. "So. Much. Family. Fun."

Josh dismisses my comment with a wave of his hand and signs the credit card receipt. Once he sees that we're three-hundred-fifty dollars lighter, Josh forgets his enthusiasm for a road trip and instead looks like he wants to put me on the Batman ride without a protective harness. It's not my fault the kids looked up at the wrong moment. He should have distracted them instead of checking his e-mail – and I totally saw the screen open to his fantasy baseball roster, so he wasn't working like he said he was going to anyway.

After waiting in interminably long lines for a few rides, the kids spy a section of carnie games and ask if they can play. "Yes, go ahead," I say. Josh stands back and motions for me to handle it. Thanks for your support, *Josh*.

"Mommy, we want to play this one!" Emmie says, gesturing to a water-gun game where contestants play against each other to see who can squirt water in a hole, filling a container the fastest. The sign says if three people play, a winner is guaranteed. Well alrighty then, let's settle up. I slap twelve dollars on the counter and the kids sit down in birth order from left to right. I offer to help Maeve aim her water gun and she screams like I am trying to kidnap her and pushes my arm away. Okay, crazy, go it alone and lose to your better-coordinated older siblings. I watch as the bell rings and the water starts spewing forth. The race is tight between Jack and Emmie, but Maeve is nowhere near the mark. I worry about her future baseball abilities; this kid can't hit the broadside of a barn based on what I see here. But in true three-year-old fashion, she really doesn't care. She thinks she's winning, so more power to her.

The other two look like they are engaged in an epic battle of skill. Emmie's tongue is poking out of the side of her mouth as she concentrates and Jack is squeezing the trigger with approximately nine hundred pounds of pressure, as if squeezing harder will make the water come out faster. They are locked in a duel to the death and I am frankly worried one of them is going to turn the gun on the other in the face of defeat.

The bell rings and Emmie jumps off her stool screaming, "I won! I won!" with her arms above her head in victory. The smile on her face is huge, but the storm cloud looming over her shoulder is bigger. Jack doesn't say a word, just launches himself over the counter and tries to grab a stuffed prize. I see this peripherally because I am picking Maeve up off the ground while she screams, "But I wanted to win! I wanted toooo winnnnn!"

Jack gets my full attention, however, when I see Josh grab him by the ankles and pull him back to the customer side of the counter. The seventeen-year-old employee is white-faced and not really sure what the appropriate course of action is here. As Jack is escorted to a nearby bench by Josh, and when I say "escorted" please know I mean "forcibly dragged kicking and screaming," Maeve is crying real tears and burying her face in my legs. Meanwhile, to the victor goes the spoils, and Emmie is proudly clutching a thirty-six-inch purple and pink stuffed beaver.

She proudly marches over to the bench where Jack is serving a six-to-twelve-month sentence for attempted theft, and starts waving the stuffed beaver in his face and singing, "I ammmmm the winnnnerrrrrr." This child has a death wish. Jack lunges for the beaver while Josh holds him down on the bench.

"Emmie! That is not nice. How would you feel if you lost and Jack won and he did that to you?" I ask.

"I don't know," she says. "But I know that I ammmmm the winnnnerrrrr!"

Ignoring her extremely poor sportsmanship, I turn my attention toward Jack, who is sobbing on the bench and squirming around trying to extricate himself from Josh's clutches. I bend down and decide to use it as a teachable moment.

"Jackie, somebody has to win and somebody has to lose," I say. "This time you lost. Another time you'll win."

"But I wanted to win today," he cries plaintively. "It's not fair."

"You're right, carnie games aren't fair, they're rigged."

"What does that mean?"

"That means they set them up so no one can win."

"But Emmie won!"

He has a point there. As I open my mouth to attempt to explain that life's not fair and this is how we learn to be gracious losers and not everybody gets a trophy just for showing up, despite what his soccer league says, I see Emmie dancing around with the beaver as a partner, swinging it to and fro like she's Fred Astaire and the beaver is Ginger Rogers. Maeve gets a load of this and declares war. She makes a grab for the beaver and Emmie, surprised, pulls back while screaming, "Maeve! No!"

Emmie might have twenty-three months on Maeve, but Maeve does not mess around when it comes to asserting her strength. I have seen this child bring Jack down from behind and pull Emmie's hair right out of the follicles. When she digs in, she digs in. And this is one of those times. Maeve sets her heels and pulls with all of her thirty pounds while Emmie (thirty-eight pounds dripping wet if she's lucky) is caught off-balance and tumbles to the ground. Maeve follows her down due to her death-grip on the beaver's purple polyester tail and the two girls are grappling on the asphalt for control of the prize. People are walking by, staring and pointing. Josh, still hanging on to Jack, looks at me and gives me the "this is your problem" look.

I separate the girls, removing the offending beaver from both of their hands. They stand up screaming and crying and I hold my hand up to signal for silence.

"Emmie, take the beaver and go stand over there," I say. "If I see you rubbing it in anyone's face again, the beaver sleeps with the fish. Maeve, you stand over here and don't move. And Jack, you make one move for that beaver the rest of the day and I will build a dam in the doorway to your bedroom so you can't get out. I have never seen such atrocious behavior from three children who were lucky enough to have their parents take them to Six Flags. We are leaving."

"Hey, hey, hey," Josh interrupts. "Let's not be so hasty. I haven't even had time to ride X-Flight yet. And for three-hundred-fifty dollars, I better get to ride the new roller coaster."

"Ahh, no. I am not taking the three of them anywhere by myself," I respond.

"You know who would let me enjoy myself on X-Flight?" Josh says. "My Canadian wife and kids. She would want me to live life to its fullest. She would allow me to do whatever I wanted. She wouldn't be saying 'yes' to our children for some ridiculous project. She would understand me."

"She is welcome to you. In fact, I encourage you to go find a Canadian wife right now. Go, go on. Flannel shirts and hockey sweaters are the new black. Maple syrup shooters for everyone! Knock yourself out. Kids, who wants to go to the lake house?"

Two of three kids cry, "I do!" In fairness, I tell the lone holdout the majority rules. The holdout takes her stuffed beaver and throws it on the ground in protest. I calmly pick it up and tuck it under my arm as we walk toward the exit. Josh trails behind, wistfully watching X-Flight as it flies above us in the distance. As we walk, I reflect on the nonsense that just occurred. I tried to be all cool and fun and laid-back and nobody gave a crap what Mommy thought. We shelled out hundreds of dollars for an excursion that resulted in fisticuffs and stares of disapproval from other people. Awesome.

As we get in the car and everyone settles back into his or her seat, Josh points his finger at me. "For your information, they don't drink maple syrup in Canada," he says. "They put it on their pancakes just like us. You're just an anti-Canadianite."

"That's not even a thing, first of all," I say, "and second of all, I love Canadians. Remember when we went to Montreal and ate our weight in smoked meat? And the time we saw Pearl Jam, there? I love Canada. I even know the words to the National Anthem."

"Oh yeah, what comes after 'Oh, Canada?'"

"I don't have to prove anything to you."

"That's because you don't know! You don't know what comes next!"

"Again, I am secure in my knowledge of Canada. I don't need to shout it from the rooftops."

"*Our home and native land! True patriot-love in all thy sons command. With glowing hearts we see thee rise, the True North strong and free! And stand on guard, O Canada, we stand on guard for thee.*" Josh sings with a booming bass voice. If there had been a Canadian flag, I think he would have wrapped himself in it.

"You are so ridiculous," I say. "And you just Googled that five seconds ago."

"There is nothing ridiculous about Canada. It's a beautiful land full of beautiful people."

"I'm sure you and your second wife and will be very happy there."

"We absolutely will. What Canadian wife wouldn't be happy with a Six Flags LaRonde pass?"

CHAPTER FIVE
I PLEAD THE FOURTH

The Fourth of July is a big holiday in our family. The day kicks off with a parade in Milwaukee's Humboldt Park, the same parade we've attended for the past thirty-five years. It's a very small production featuring a couple of floats, school groups with kids on bikes and parents pulling tricked-out wagons, some fire trucks and convertibles containing local news celebrities and politicians. People throw candy from floats and kids scramble off the curb to grab as much as their tiny hands will handle. It's wholesome Wisconsin fun.

This morning, my parents arrived at the park at the ass-crack of dawn to secure a good spot for our group. No lie, my mom proudly tells me they were the first people there. At six-forty-five a.m. Good lord, woman, I'm not sure the people sitting five feet to the left of us have a terrible view of the festivities and they got there around eight-ten for the nine-fifteen start. But I graciously thank her for getting things secured as I crack open a cold bottle of water in my lawn chair. Grandma Mary and Grandpa Dave always come prepared.

Jack, Emmie and Maeve sit down near the curb so they have maximum exposure to the candy debris field, which raises my heart rate into aerobic territory every time a moving vehicle slowly rolls by because I'm afraid they will run out and be crushed under a pickup-truck trailed by a float. Jack has amassed an impressive pile of Tootsie Rolls and Starbursts and Emmie is unwrapping and eating Smarties as fast as her hands will move. Maeve has been working on a butterscotch-flavored Dum Dums sucker for quite some time, which means she's ignoring the rest of the candy, which is fine by me.

"They should totally pick us as the parade emcees next year," my sister, Beth, announces. "We'd be way funnier than this dude."

"Seriously," I say. "I mean come on, this is ripe for the snark. How do you let an Elvis impersonator go by without yelling, 'Elvis has left the building' and screaming like a girl?"

"I picture us doing a whole 'Survivor-style' bit, announcing live on the loudspeaker whether each group will be invited back for next year's parade," Beth says.

"I can see it now. Next up, we have the Leslynette Twirlers. Cassidy, their lead twirler, isn't with them today after a nasty incident with a flaming baton and a French braid. But first-runner-up, Charlotte, is really giving us all she's got. Ooooohhhhhh, that was some bad luck there, Charlotte, boinking the baton off the top of your noggin. We're going to have to ask you turn in your parade credentials. You won't be welcome back next year."

Beth picks up where I leave off. "And next up, we have Miss South Shore Water Frolic, Britteney Colochowski. Britteney, your daddy's convertible Mazda Miata is pretty sweet, but 1989 called and it wants its car back. And Britteney? You're not performing a regulation beauty-contestant wave, you're just swinging your arm around wildly. You'll need to exit the parade route immediately, you're done."

Beth nearly jumps out of her skin as a World War I re-enactment quartet fires a rifle into the air ten feet behind her. Teenage boys rush to gather the shells off the asphalt while my sister, now deaf in both ears, screams, "We're back in 'Nam! Take cover! Incoming!" and rolls to the side of the blanket she's sitting on. My brother-in-law, Kevin, sighs and tells her to stop embarrassing him.

"You're embarrassed about my service to my country?" she yells. "I was there when Saigon fell. I know what it means to lose a fellow brother in the field. I liberated women and children in small Vietnamese villages."

"Just stop," he says, tossing their daughter, Lylah, in the air above his head and catching her as she laughs. "You sound ridiculous. Please, the closest you've ever come to a battlefield is Walmart on Black Friday and eating Vietnamese food one time does not count as liberating women and children."

Beth rolls to a seated position and salutes the tiny American flag Emmie is waving. I am laughing so hard I can't catch my breath and Josh is ignoring all of us and playing a video game on his phone. Another float rolls by and when they toss the candy, a Now and Later hits me in the head and bounces off me.

"I'm hit!" I yell, "I'm hit!"

Beth army-crawls across the blanket to where I am slumped in my lawn chair. "It's bad," she says seriously. "Schrapnel in your forehead. We might have to do a field amputation."

"I've always said she needed a head amputation," Josh interjects. "It can only improve her intelligence level from where it is now."

"No, save yourself!" I yell, ignoring him. "I will only slow you down."

"I will never leave you behind. Semper Fi!"

Kevin is now so annoyed with us he moves down near the kids on the curb. We're hilarious, he's just jealous we're funnier than he is. We manage to stop giggling as one of the last floats, a paper-mache Statue of Liberty in front of a giant tissue-papered American flag, makes its way past our spot, the song, "God Bless The USA," blasting from a pair of old-school speakers in the back of the pickup truck. My dad yells, "Who wants ice cream?" and all the kids scramble to follow him. It's also a family tradition to jump in the back of the parade and grab a free ice cream. Hey, my parents pay taxes, they earned that ice cream.

The kids return scraping vanilla ice cream out of Styrofoam cups with little wooden paddles – nothing like candy followed by ice cream at ten-thirty in the morning – and we pack up to leave. My in-laws, Scott and Marilee, are also in attendance and we all make plans to head to a nearby Perkins for brunch. After overseeing the negotiations over who rides in what car, Josh and I revel in the silence of our empty SUV. Shockingly, they are able to seat a party of twelve on a moment's notice and we are quickly ready to order. I'm sitting as far away from the children as possible, which is easy with so many grandparents on hand, when I hear Jack ask my mother-in-law, Marilee, if he can have orange juice.

"Of course," she says enthusiastically.

"And bacon?" he adds hopefully.

"Yes," she says, fielding a hug from the happiest child on earth.

I shoot her a look down the table and she smiles back. What the hell? Our kids don't drink juice, period. And the grandmas know it. And unless that pig was raised on a local farm foraging for plants and table scraps, bacon isn't on the approved list, either.

She busies herself playing a rousing game of Tic-Tac-Toe with Jack until the food comes, while I try to ignore the outside voices being used at the table. Under normal circumstances, I would have shushed them a thousand times and told them to knock it off, but not this month. Sorry, fellow Perkins diners, you picked the wrong month to try proving the slogan that "Breakfast is Just the Beginning." More like the beginning of the end of your sanity with children yelling at the top of their lungs.

Maeve gets up out of her seat and starts twirling in the aisle. I shoot Josh an exasperated look and ask him to deal with her. "No way, this is your thing, don't make me the bad guy," he says, taking a long drink of my orange juice. Why can't he just get his own?

"Maevie, could you please sit down?" I ask nicely. She ignores me. This time I tell her. "Maeve, please find a chair and put your butt on it." Of course, that sets her off into hysterical laughter.

"Butt butt butt," she sings. "Shake your booty, shake your booty." Her singing is accompanied by butt-shaking and hip-smacking, and the other two now feel compelled to join in. Jack is dancing like Elaine from *Seinfeld*, and like Elaine, I don't think he's being ironic. His arms are flailing and he's sticking his butt out in an exaggerated fashion, smacking himself on the rear. This kid needs a hip-hop class, stat. The one who *is* enrolled in hip-hop class, however, might need to be un-enrolled after the moves I see her busting out. Hips gyrating, arms above her head – it will be a miracle if she doesn't end up on a pole someday. The grandparents are having a grand time watching this little spectacle and make no moves to corral anyone into a nearby seat.

"Guys," I begin, pinching the bridge of my nose between my thumb and forefinger, "I need you to please sit down and stop reenacting *Club MTV* in the middle of Perkins."

"What's MTV?" Jack asks, still slapping his own butt.

"It was a channel on TV when I was growing up that played music videos," I said.

"Oh, like YouTube?" he asks.

"Yes. No. Kind of. Never mind. Oh look, pancakes are here!"

Saved by the waitress, the kids immediately move to their seats and start grabbing for butter and syrup. Jack asks if he can pour his own syrup and Grandma Martsi hands him the container, which he pours half of onto his plate. His pancakes are no longer visible because they are drowned in a sea of chemicals manipulated to smell and taste like maple syrup, but which we all know contains not a trace of actual maple syrup. As he brings forkful after forkful to his mouth, he dribbles gobs of syrup down the front of his blue Old Navy flag-adorned shirt. Good thing that was only five bucks and doesn't need to be worn again.

Emmie is eating her bacon like a cartoon beaver eats a piece of wood. She's like a wood chipper, shoving bacon in and speedily shredding it in her mouth. She finishes her order and asks Grandma Martsi for a piece of hers, which she gladly hands over. Emmie's eyes practically roll back in her head in ecstasy.

"Mommy!" she yells down the table. "This bacon is delicious! I want to have it every day." Perhaps you should bring this up with your pediatric cardiologist next year, as that's the road you're heading down with this diet, missy.

Maeve is literally eating syrup with a fork. She's abandoned all pretense of using a piece of pancake as a vehicle for the syrup and is just dipping and re-dipping her fork, licking the brown gooeyness off the utensil. I ask her to eat some of her pancakes and she shoots me daggers with her eyes, staring straight at me, delicately licking each individual tine of the fork.

I turn my attention to my own waffle with berries and whipped cream and try to block out the nonsense at the other end of the table. As I bring my fork to my mouth, I hear Jack ask Beth if he can have some of her French fries. "Of course you can have some of my French fries," she says exaggeratedly. "In fact, you can have them all and I will get another order." She smirks in my direction and passes the plate right across me.

"You will pay for this," I hiss, grabbing her wrist and twisting. She wrenches her arm away and smiles malevolently. "Wanna bet?" she retorts to me, before telling Jack, "Just let me know if you want more."

As I turn my head, I catch a glimpse of Emmie and the waitress out of the corner of my eye and almost fall out of my chair as I see the waitress placing a second large glass of orange juice in front of Emmie.

"Emily!" I say, as she quickly starts gulping it down. "What on earth are you doing?"

Gasping for air between gulps, she says, "Grandma said I could."

My sister is convulsing with laughter and manages to drag the ends of her hair through the ketchup on her plate. I'm not even going to point that out, instead letting her go about her day with dried tomato product in her hair. Serves her right that she's going to smell like a barbecue all day.

We manage to get ourselves to the lobby without a major international incident where I corner Marilee away from the children. "What was that?" I ask, jamming my thumb back toward the table.

"What? I thought since it was Yes Mommy month, it was Yes Grandma month, too," she says innocently.

"It's been Yes Grandma month for the last seven years," I say in exasperation. "No more, it's not funny."

"Whatever you say … " she trails off and gestures to the bakery case where all three kids are gathered with their noses pressed flat on the glass, their breath steaming up the clean glass. My mother is standing behind them asking what they all want.

"I want chocolate chip," Jack yells. Emmie asks for oatmeal raisin, because she's awesome, and Maeve wants M&M. My mom buys them each two cookies and happily doles them out.

"Mom! What the hell are you doing?" I ask.

"What? They need one for each hand."

I give her a dirty look, tamping down my urge to flip her off (and don't only because she's my mother) and flounce out of the restaurant to the parking lot. Beth and Kevin come out with the infant car seat, laughing and pointing at me.

"Oh, you just wait," I said. "Lylah is a baby now, but this is coming back to you in spades."

"Oh yeah? What could you possibly do to her that we won't? We let our kids eat ice cream, French fries, candy, whatever. We bring meat home from the grocery store and actually inject it with extra hormones for flavor. There's nothing you could do to top that."

"Oh yeah? Well guess what? I'm going to feed her free-range pork and milk from grass-fed cows and for dessert, we're going to have organic strawberries."

My sister gasps. "You wouldn't dare!" My sister, although an educated woman, truly doesn't believe organic products are better for you and actually goes out of her way to *not* eat organic, just to prove her point.

"Watch me," I cackle.

My victory is short-lived, however, when my children spill out onto the hot asphalt, covered in crumbs and chocolate. Maeve holds out her hand and says solemnly, "Mommy, I got chocolate on my hands," thus disproving the theory that M&Ms melt in your mouth, not in your hands.

After yet another argument about who rides in which car – a matter I smartly stay out of – we settle in for the childless ride home and I turn on Josh.

"What the hell was that with your mother?" I ask.

"I have no idea. But what the hell with your mom, too?" he replies.

"Right? That was crazy. Two cookies. Who the hell gives a kid two cookies?"

"Apparently, your mother. But in her defense, she also bought me two cookies." Josh holds up a white waxed-paper bag with a smile.

"And who the hell gives a kid carte blanche with the bacon and the orange juice?" I ask.

"Yeah, that was crazy. Bacon and orange juice. We're lucky she didn't try to add eggs in to the mix! I'm just glad we escaped with our lives!"

"Listen, funny man, lots of moms don't let their kids drink juice. It's pure sugar with no fiber. You want some juice? Suck it out of the whole orange while you eat it. And bacon? They might as well call it 'cancer sticks' with all the nitrates and chemicals they add."

"Well at least my mom is the one who has to deal with the sugar-crash on the way home!"

This is where normal couples might high-five, but Josh and I have a strict "no-high-fiving policy," something we share with our good friends, Gina and Jeff. The only people who should ever be high-fiving are baseball players at home plate after a home run and babies. And even the babies might be questionable after the age of two. In fact, Gina is so anti-high-five that she refused to teach her daughter the move. That's hardcore, right there.

Instead we nod our heads in silence and turn up the Radiohead CD in our car. Yes, we're still stuck with CDs because our 2003 car doesn't have satellite radio or an MP3 jack. We're old-school like that. We might as well have an eight-track, as far as I'm concerned, but Josh doesn't believe getting a new car just for the music capabilities is a good enough reason. He clearly hates me.

When we arrive back at the lake house, I'm able to Yes Mommy Maeve into taking a nap – I love it when they scream no and I smile and quietly say yes – and I take my iPad out onto the deck to read. Jack and Emmie wander out wearing swimsuits and life jackets and ask if they can go down and jump off the end of the dock. "Yes, yes you can," I say, adding, "And ask your grandmother to go with you."

Evil, I know, but she asked for that one with that nonsense Yes Grandma move.

CHAPTER SIX
CEREAL KILLERS

Someone is whispering to me in my dream, but I can't quite figure out what the person is saying. Something about milk, I think. If this mystery person would only speak up, I could figure it out. I realize it's no dream when a tiny warm hand smacks my cheek repeatedly. My eyes open to a mess of blonde ringlets and a pair of big blue eyes approximately two inches from my face. "Mommy, I want some milk," the ringlet-headed girl whispers loudly. It's five-fifty-five in the morning, isn't it a little early for this? I close my eyes and a hand pats the top of my head. "Mommy? Mommy! Wake up! I want some milk," Maeve says again, right up in my grill.

I sigh and throw the duvet back and sit on the side of the bed for a moment, trying to get my bearings. Maeve tugs on my arm and I reluctantly leave my bed. I follow this small dictator as she drags her green fuzzy blanket behind her down the stairs and into the kitchen. One would think dictators would dress more formally than polka-dot baby doll pajamas with ladybugs on the front – they might get more respect that way. But Maeve the Malevolent cares nothing of appearances. I open the cabinet and randomly grab a purple Dora the Explorer sippy cup, a yellow lid and spend precious seconds searching for one of those stupid flexible plastic insert things so it won't leak all over the place. I finally find one and pour the milk into the cup, screw the lid in place and hand it to her.

"Nooooooooooo!" she screams, throwing herself on the hardwood floor. "I don't want that cup. I want the flower one."

"Maeve, this is ridiculous," I hiss. "It's a cup. It has milk in it. It's six o'clock in the morning. I am not arguing over the cup. Take it or leave it."

"I want the flower one!" she yells.

"No!" I yell back. And then I stop myself. Wait. Through the haze of exhaustion I realize we're in the throes of Operation Yes Mommy.

"Fine? You want the flower cup? Here you go." I grab a different cup and lid assembly out of the cabinet and pour the milk from the Dora cup into the flower-covered cup. I hand her the cup, my eyes most certainly flashing anger.

"Tank you," she says through her tears. She pads over to the couch in the living room and sits down. "I want to watch *Yo Gabba Gabba*." Silently, I cue up the video as she gets settled on the couch. I turn around to put the remote down and find another small blonde child sitting on the couch with a pink fuzzy blanket.

"Hi, Mommy," Emmie says. "I'm awake."

Thank you, Captain Obvious. I hand Emmie the remote and head back upstairs. The best thing that ever happened to my parenting was when I realized the kids could watch videos while I went back to sleep. With the amount of tattling in this house, we're kept informed of all breaking news on the behavior front and because both Jack and Emmie know how to read and operate the remote, they handle the cueing up of the videos and we go back to bed. It's genius.

I pass Jack at the top of the steps and he takes the stairs two at a time to get down to the television as quickly as possible. I crawl under the covers and fall back asleep. It's not even ten minutes before someone is at my bedside again.

"Mommy? Can I have some cheese?" Emmie asks.

"Yes," I say, not opening my eyes.

"Yes!" she says, raising her arms in victory and running back downstairs. This yes thing is working out beautifully.

Two minutes later Jack is yelling up the stairs, "Can we have a breakfast picnic?"

Breakfast picnic started when we let the kids pour dry cereal into Ziploc baggies and eat it in front of the TV. Weekends are primetime for breakfast picnic, as it allows Mommy and Daddy even more time to sleep because no one is screaming for food. And the kids think it's the greatest thing ever. It never ceases to amaze me that my kids will eat anything if it's contained in a baggie. Hand Maeve a piece of broccoli and she will act like you're trying to kill her. Put that same piece of broccoli in a Ziploc bag and she'll ask for fifteen more pieces. But breakfast picnic tends to devolve into "throw the cereal on the floor and grind it into the couch fabric" so we've severely curtailed its use lately. Until today.

"Yep, knock yourself out," I tell Jack.

"Emmie! Emmie! Mommy said we can have breakfast picnic!" Jack yells downstairs. I hear whooping. It's the little things.

Within a minute, a little face is next to mine again. Seriously, I just want some sleep. Is that too much to ask at six-twenty in the morning?

"Mommy? Jack is having bwekfist picnic," Maeve reports.

"Yes, I know," I say. "I told him he could."

"Jaaaaaack! I want bwekfist picnic, too!" she screams from my bedside. Unfortunately, Maeve doesn't yet grasp the dynamics of sound waves.

"What?" Jack yells up the stairs.

"I! Want! Bwekfist! Picnic!" Maeve yells back, emphasizing each (wrong) syllable.

"Maevie, you can totally have breakfast picnic if you just go downstairs," I say. "Please, Mommy is very tired."

"No, I want *you* to get my bwekfist picnic," she whines.

I sigh, throwing back the covers. I go downstairs, grab a handful of organic Honey Os cereal, throw them in a Ziploc bag and hand it to Maeve, who happily sits down on the couch and starts munching. I go back to bed. All is well and I fall back asleep.

I wander back downstairs around seven-forty-five to find the children have purchased a new rug and had it delivered in the time I was upstairs. At least I think it's a new rug because our old one was gray and this one is tan with a distinct circle pattern. In fact, it looks suspiciously like a rug covered in Honey Os. Probably because it *is* a rug covered in Honey Os. But not just Honey Os. No, there's also mini peanut-butter sandwich crackers and tortilla chips on the floor. Someone sure took some literary freedom with his definition of "breakfast picnic." Honey Os have questionable health value to begin with, but the addition of the other two items pretty much takes it into "junk-food picnic" territory.

"What happened here?" I ask loudly, looking down from the stairs. All three children jump when they hear my voice.

"Mommy, you scared me!" Emmie says. That was kind of the point, Em.

"And I'm scared by all the cereal on the floor," I reply.

"Jack did that," she and Maeve say simultaneously. The tattle gene is strong in this family.

"I did not," Jack says, trying to defend himself. "It was Maeve and Emmie! I ate all mine."

I tend to believe him in this instance, seeing as a growing boy never leaves food uneaten. It's a basic tenant of life, right up there with breathing and sleeping.

"Look, somebody needs to clean this mess up," I say. "This is why I didn't want to let you have breakfast picnic. But I was nice and I said yes. So somebody needs to clean up this mess if you want to be able to do it ever again."

Emmie slithers off the couch into a heap on the floor and Maeve rolls over on her back with the iPad, ignoring me. And then the strangest thing happens. Emmie starts picking up the cereal, one organic Honey O by one organic Honey O and putting them in her mouth. Do my eyes deceive me? Is she willingly cleaning up this mess? Be still my heart. Hey, five-second rule, five-minute rule, whatever – my floor is being cleaned despite whatever dirt she might be ingesting.

"Maeve! Help me clean up or Mommy won't let us have breakfast picnic anymore," Emmie scolds, duckwalking across the carpet picking up cereal. Maeve rolls again, this time crushing Honey Os under her back as she does so. That's gonna leave a mark. Emmie screams, "Maeve! Stop it! I am trying to clean!" Well, well, well – someone knows what it feels like to issue directives and have them blatantly ignored. Maeve scoops a handful of cereal off the floor and for a millisecond I believe she's going to help, but that belief is shattered when she chucks the handful of Honey Os at Emmie and gleefully laughs.

"Maeve! No! Stop it!" Shockingly, these words aren't coming from my own mouth, but from Emmie's. This is beautiful. She starts to cry, which is my cue to step in.

"Maeve, that wasn't nice," I say. "Emmie is trying to clean up and you're making her upset. Please either help out or go to another room." Unsurprisingly, she takes her iPad down to the basement playroom. Well, at least she's no longer throwing cereal at her sister. Emmie is still upset, moaning how it's not fair that she's cleaning up all by herself. But she's doing it. Eventually, she grabs a baggie and cleans up all three-thousand-seven-hundred-and-twenty-nine Os by herself and dumps the bag in the garbage. I thank her profusely while she continues to make her displeasure known.

"Mommy, no one was listening to me!" she whines. "I was cleaning up and no one was helping."

Never one to miss a teachable moment, I jump right in.

"Now you know what Mommy feels like when no one listens," I say. "I don't like cleaning up messes by myself, either. Now that you know how it feels, what do you think you should do about it?"

Emmie levels her gaze at me and says with great seriousness, "Well I am never going to be a mommy, that's for sure. I am not cleaning up messes every day."

CHAPTER SEVEN
THEY ALL SCREAM FOR ICE CREAM

We're more than a week in and I'm still not batting a thousand on saying yes. In fact, I would be hard-pressed to make a high-school freshman B-team baseball team with my average, which hovers disturbingly in the low two-hundreds by my best estimate. Not a single day has gone by where I haven't uttered one of the words "no, don't, stop," although I do quickly correct myself. But I have hit the point where I at least respond to direct requests with "yes." Can I have another snack? Yes. Can we go out for pizza? Yes. Can I go to Grandma's house and sleep over? Absolutely, let me find a suitcase and dial the phone for you.

The trickiest situations are the ones that involve questionable behavior rather than requests for action. I am happy to let them watch another video, but when you start beating the bananas out of your sister because she has the iPad and you want it? Well that's not as easy to handle. As a parent, there are so many situations where your first instinct is to say no. Walk into a room and find your seven-year-old dangling his little sister by the ankles off the couch, and you just automatically yell, "No!" without thinking. But at least I'm self-correcting.

For instance, after showers and teeth-brushing tonight, Emmie sidles up to me. "Can I have dessert?" she asks sweetly. Exasperated as I yell down the hall for Jack to stop wasting all the hot water and get in the shower already, I turn back to her. "Emmie, you're in your pajamas and already brushed your teeth. We're not having dessert now." Her face crumples as I remember my pledge, so I change my answer on the fly. "But if you really want it, sure, let's do it."

She smiles brightly and clasps her hands together under her chin with a sneaky smile. "I want to go get ice cream at Baskin Robbins!"

I stare at her for a moment, wondering if someone has told her about the experiment. She has a gift for sensing weakness, this one. I sigh and say, "Sure. Get your shoes." She flies down the stairs and I ask Josh to strong-arm a naked Maeve into her Hello Kitty pajamas and continue harassing Jack to get in the damn shower already. Our water bills are astronomical.

"Why, where are you going?" he asks, not looking up from his phone. He's wearing his Jonathan Toews Blackhawks jersey, which I refuse to even acknowledge. Toews, one of the squad's captains, is Canadian and helped his country to a gold medal in the last Olympics. Of course he did. Josh is just begging to start a discourse about this, but I refuse to engage. If he wants to wear a hockey sweater in the midst of a heatwave, that's his problem. But it's not like he's taking any big fashion risks – the Hawks won the Stanley Cup a few short weeks ago and all of Chicago is still sporting Blackhawks gear in pride.

"Emmie asked to go to Baskin Robbins," I say.

"This is insane, she's in her pajamas and it's bedtime," he points out.

"I agree. And yet, we're still going."

"I think I should take her."

"Why would you take her?"

"This is the most hectic half-hour of the day. I have to wrestle two crazies into the shower, then into pajamas, brush their hair and teeth, and finally get them in bed while you're off eating ice cream? Are you serious? This doesn't sound like Yes Mommy to me, it sounds more like Screw Daddy."

"I'm going to have one kid with me, it's not like I'm going by myself."

"One? One kid is like a vacation. One kid isn't going to lick someone else's cone. One kid doesn't whine about not having the biggest scoop. One kid doesn't fight with itself."

"Well Yes Mommy is going to Baskin Robbins with Emmie," I say, sighing. I don't need his nonsense on top of everything else.

"Fantastic. I guess Screw Daddy will just be here putting Maeve to bed. And Screw Daddy wants a pint of mint chocolate chip."

Emmie waltzes in to the ice cream store like she owns the place. A middle-aged man and his wife are enjoying a cup of coffee and smile when they see her coming. With her wet hair, striped shorty pajamas and sandals, she's a vision. She walks slowly in front of the ice cream case, reading the names of all the flavors. When she sees rainbow sherbet, she squeals.

"Mommy, I want rainbow!" she yells. The man behind the counter grabs a scoop and she adds, "on a cone" so he grabs a cake cone and places the scoop on it and hands it to her. She happily licks it as we stand at the register when she stops and looks at me.

"Mommy, can I have a doughnut, too?" she asks hopefully. This is both the beauty and the danger of a combination Dunkin Donuts/Baskin

Robbins – choices. Normally, I'm a pick your poison kind of gal: you get either a doughnut or an ice cream. What kind of idiot parent allows them to have both? Today, it's this idiot parent.

"Sure," I say through gritted teeth. "Whatever you want."

Emmie almost drops the cone she is so surprised with her good fortune. She quickly asks the cashier for a chocolate long john and he bags one up on the spot. Of course she chose the biggest doughnut she could get her hands on. Go big or go home, right?

When she asks if we can eat it there, I am happy to say yes because it means the other two-thirds of the small people in my life won't have to know about it. She is beside herself with her good fortune, alternating licks of her ice cream and bites of her doughnut. She has a chocolate moustache and a smear of pink and green slime on her cheek, but is chattering happily about her upcoming camp field trip to Pump It Up, a warehouse of bounce houses.

Mid-lick, she stops and inspects a drop of orange sherbet on her leg. She wipes it up with her index finger and licks it. She points to her groin and says, "I know what this is called."

"Your leg?" I ask. I hope she knows what her leg is called, we mastered that skill back when she was a year-and-a-half old.

"No, your leg *pit*," she says, with great seriousness.

"I'm sorry, what?" I ask.

"You know, this is your arm pit," she says, pointing to her underarm, "so this is your leg pit."

Damned if she isn't technically right. I go to the counter to grab some more napkins so she doesn't see me laughing.

She savors every bite of both her cone and the long john and every moment of alone time with me before reluctantly heading back to the car. She is practically levitating she is so happy. That, or she is actually levitating thanks to the amount of sugar she just ingested. It's hard to tell.

We get home and I instruct her to brush her teeth for a second time. I let her squeeze the berry-flavored kid's toothpaste on her pink electric toothbrush and let her go about her business before taking a turn to make sure she doesn't miss any spots. After she finishes, she jumps off the stool and runs right to Maeve's room, where Maeve is reading a Mo Willems book with Josh.

"Maeve! Guess where I just got to go!" she exclaims. My first reaction is to yell, "Noooooooooo" in super slow motion, but she's quicker than I am, even if I was allowed to say no in the first place. "Mommy took me to Baskin Robbins and I got to have ice cream *and* a doughnut!"

Josh looks at me incredulously as I try to come up with a plan to refute this information to Maeve. "You didn't think they would talk?" he asks. "This isn't a prison, you know. It's not like they only get to mingle with the general population once a day. Although, that's not a bad idea. We should look into implementing something like that."

Emmie stands there just willing Maeve to punch her in the face. The problem with instigating jealousy amongst siblings at this young age is that they haven't learned to curb actual violent outbursts yet. Don't like the fact your sister just came home with a new toy? Well just smack the freckles off her face and see how she likes the toy then. The nuanced retort, a combination of insult and sarcasm, is still years away. I know, as I perfected that skill on my own sister during my teenage years. Predictably, Maeve flies into a rage.

"I want ice cream and a doughnut," she screams, tears already springing to her eyes.

"Too bad for you, you can't have any," Emmie says, turning on her heel and hightailing it out of there before Maeve can get a hold of a hunk of blonde hair. Josh looks at me and puts his hands up in a self-defense gesture, indicating this is all me. Maeve screams louder and throws herself backward, hitting her head on the back of her daybed, causing her to become even more pissed off. If Emmie was standing anywhere near her, I would fear for her physical safety. Maeve can throw down, she isn't cowed by the age difference.

"Fine, come on," I say to Maeve.

She stops crying. "What you say?" she asks suspiciously.

"I said let's go. Get your shoes."

"Wait, what?" Josh exclaims. "What is going on here? Did you at least get *me* ice cream?"

"No."

"Then that settles it. It truly is Screw Daddy night. That's okay, I don't even like American ice cream, I prefer the Canadian variety."

"I'm sure there's a *huge* difference."

"Oh, there's a huge difference, all right."

"Really, what's that?"

"Well when I'm in Canada eating Canadian ice cream you aren't around driving me insane."

Not giving me a chance to change my mind, Maeve jumps off the bed and tugs on my arm. I follow along as she runs to the stairs as fast as her stocky toddler legs will allow. Josh yells after me, "That was mint chocolate chip for me, in case you forgot," and I flip him off over my shoulder as I walk down the hall. Thankfully, Jack has the bathroom door closed and for once, I hope that whatever he is doing in there keeps him occupied for a very long time.

When I return to Baskin Robbins with a second child in pajamas, this one a smaller version with dimples, the cashier gives me a quizzical look. I just shrug in response. Maeve asks for rainbow sherbet (of course she did) and a sprinkle-covered doughnut hole. Like her sister, she is ecstatic at her good fortune. Sitting there with her wet curls and her shorty pajamas, she chatters happily, giving me a running commentary. "I am eating ice cream!" she says. You don't say? Unlike her sister, however, she knows her limits and pushes back from the table with a half-full dish of melting sherbet and a doughnut hole intact, save for the tiny bites that removed every last sprinkle from the outside. She asks to go home and I gratefully clean her sticky hands and sprinkle-stained face.

Unlike some people (cough cough, Emmie), Maeve is content to get her way and drop it. Emmie is the one who insists on getting her way and then enjoying every last second of her victory. She would sooner not win at all than win and have her victory cut short. At this point, I wonder how long it will be before I am back for a third late-night ice cream run and it makes me weary. I am already gearing up for the confrontation with Jack and I haven't even had it yet. But I know it's coming.

We get home and Jack meets me at the top of the stairs. Here we go, I knew it. I hold my hand up before he can even say a word, but he ignores my nonverbal cues. "Mommy, Emmie says she got to go for ice cream and a doughnut. Is that true, Mommy? Did she really?" he asks suspiciously.

Emmie is dancing around behind Jack, singing, "I got ice cream, I got ice cream" and shaking her butt in some bizarre dance move that looks like a cross between something Sir Mix-A-Lot would endorse and a hula girl. Whatever it is, it's going to make Jack lose his marbles in about ten seconds if she doesn't knock it off.

"Yes, she went for ice cream," I say.

Maeve pipes up behind me. "And I got to go, too! I got wainbow ice cweam in a dish and a doughnut with spwinkles!" Seriously, why doesn't she just hand him a bat and invite him to beat her with it?

"Did you get any ice cream for Daddy?" Josh asks.

"Nope." I reply. "Daddy only likes Canadian ice cream, remember?"

"Why can't I go for ice cream?" Jack asks, genuinely confused as to how on earth this has happened to him. But my brain, still numb from the cool of the ice cream shop, notes he did not actually ask *if* he could go.

"Because you got to have popsicles at camp today," I point out. Hooray for telltale red cherry stains on shirts. I didn't see him eat it, but I darn well saw the mess he made of his shirt with it. It's hard to be secretive when you're a sloppy eater.

He thinks about it for a minute. "Oh, yeah, I forgot," he admits. "Can I go for ice cream and a doughnut by myself tomorrow then?"

Wait, what? I expected a scene, a huge fight, gnashing of teeth and rending of garments.

"Yes, yes you can," I tell him, startled at how easy that just was. Satisfied, he walks back into his room while I brush Maeve's teeth again.

Huh. I would have predicted a huge fight, crying and yelling and "it's not fairs" uttered in howling moans. Instead, I get a child with self-imposed limits and the patience to wait his turn until a more suitable time. This is unprecedented! This is my child who counts the number of cheddar bunnies everyone receives in a snack bowl, the child who measures the milk levels in cups, the child who once complained his sister's jump rope was slightly longer than his. For him to just accept a perceived injustice and move on? I must be doing something right with this yes thing.

I climb up into his loft bed to read the second *Harry Potter* book with him and he snuggles up next to me. Freshly washed and clad in red and black skateboard-covered pajamas, he is happy, no trace of drama about the ice cream. After we finish the chapter, he wants confirmation I remember he gets to go another time. I assure him I remember.

"You know, Mommy, I didn't need to go for ice cream today because I had a popsicle and that wasn't really healthy," he says.

Be still my heart: my child has internalized our food beliefs. Granted, the other two just gleefully consumed more sugar, fat and artificial coloring in one sitting than the recommended daily allowance, but one of our children is making the connection.

CHAPTER EIGHT
SHOWDOWN AT THE WHOLE FOODS CORRAL

You know those people who plan their meals out weeks in advance, coordinating store lists and schedules? The ones who wear aprons emblazoned with the words "Kiss the Cook!" and genuinely look forward to Taco Tuesdays and Saturday Sloppy Joes? The ones who have a fully-stocked pantry, grouped into like sections and alphabetized? And freezers full of clearly labeled packages containing everything from ground beef to chicken breasts to veal shanks? I am not one of those people.

Sure, I have a well-stocked pantry. I actually have two, one of which is located in a bathroom off the kitchen. That's right, we have a food pantry in our bathroom. When your house was built in the 1800s and you don't have any closets on your first floor, you get creative with your storage space, okay? Besides, we have rules. Like no open food containers in the bathroom pantry. We're not savages. But the double pantry system presents its own set of challenges, like double and triple purchases of some things and none of others. I went to the store several times over the last few weeks thinking we needed the casarecce noodles the kids love in my homemade chicken soup. Except I kept putting the boxes away in different spots, so I eventually amassed a collection of five different boxes of organic casarecce noodles. But then I opened the freezer to get out the chicken and found there was no chicken. The first step is recognizing you have a problem.

I make homemade meals most nights. I like to cook and, frankly, taking three kids out to a restaurant is more work than creating something. But I am rarely prepared for these meals in advance. I don't mind making several trips to the grocery store each week, because I can usually schedule it where I have one child (or sometimes zero children) with me. But today was one of those days where things got away from me. At 5:30, the kids were whining they were starving and we didn't have the ingredients for anything appetizing. Fortunately, our Whole Foods is not only a grocery store, but has a food court that rivals that of any suburban mall. I tell the children, who are seriously acting as if they have been denied food for weeks on end, to get their shoes because we're going to the store.

"I don't wanna go to the store," Jack whines.

"And I don't wanna get up early in the morning to make breakfast for you," I reply. "But I do. Now get your shoes. If everyone behaves, we can get pizza."

My pronouncement is met with great excitement and shoes are instantly procured and shoved on feet. Maeve puts hers on the wrong feet, but refuses to believe this and stubbornly tells me, "No they're not." I could tell her the sun rises in the east and this one would deny it to the death, just to be contrary. I can't wait until she's fifteen. I herd the small folk into the car and we head out. I explain that we will order the pizza and then do the shopping so as to maximize efficiency. "Maxize fishies?" Maeve asks. Something like that.

We trek through the store, all the way to the very back corner, to order the pizza. Chaos immediately breaks out when Jack says he wants basil on top and Emmie argues she doesn't. He shoves her, she falls and howls in protest. I give him a look of death and he laughs as I help her up and hug her. "Do you think that was nice?" I ask him angrily. "How would you like it if someone did that to you?"

"I would like it very much," he says, laughing inappropriately and spinning around.

"Can I push the cart, Mommy?" Jack asks. Shit. It's primetime at the grocery store. Twenty-somethings are wandering the aisles in their professional clothes, couples strolling leisurely with a glass of wine in hand, perusing the olive bar and the fifty-four-dollar-per-pound cheeses. This is no time for a seven-year-old to crash the cart into the back of anyone's stiletto. But out of my mouth comes the magic word: yes.

"But, you have to be very careful and stay right with me and not bang it into anyone," I say. "Do you hear me?"

Of course he hears me, but does he internalize it? No. No he does not. Because the words are no sooner out of my mouth than he is careening down the aisle with Maeve in the big basket part of the cart and Emmie hanging on to the front. I should never have taken them out in public this month.

"Guys! Seriously! Watch out!" I am getting dirty looks from every hipster in the bulk grains section. A bearded man with heavy, dark-framed glasses actually jumps out of the way of the cart and I quickly apologize and hiss, "Jack! Be careful!" Of course he doesn't hear me because he is in the next aisle treating it as his own Indianapolis Speedway. I catch up to them when they pause at a free sample of popcorn.

"Mommy! Popcorn! Can we have some?" they ask in unison.

This is where I employ my new favorite strategy that has evolved out of this month: the "yes, but." This is beautiful for so many different reasons, the best being it allows me to get away with kind of saying no. Can I have a third dessert? Yes, but ... it would make your tummy hurt. Can I stay up late? Yes, but ... you won't be able to go on your field trip to Pump It Up tomorrow if you're tired. So I employ it now.

"Yes, you can have popcorn, but ... you won't be able to push the cart and eat at the same time," I point out. Jack happily relinquishes the cart and shoves his hand straight into the communal bowl of popcorn. Never mind the tongs placed in the bowl specifically so no one would do this, it's cool. Emmie and Maeve take their own turns before the floor around the bowl is covered with popcorn detritus. It looks like it snowed in aisle six. But I have won the cart battle, which is the important part.

We cruise over to the deli to grab some shaved turkey breast. For this price, the turkey better have been raised in someone's living room and fed flakes of gold. While we're waiting for the man to carve the sandwich meat off the breast, Emmie asks if she can eat the ice pellets out of a nearby display holding bottles of lemonade. Oh my god, what? Are you kidding me? That's disgusting. I've read the studies about restaurant ice being more germ-filled than toilet water. And no one is sticking his grubby hands in the restaurant ice machine to grab a bottle of lemonade. I mentally calculate the medical co-pays and deductibles for an emergency room visit for three kids with gastrointestinal distress. It seems like an opportune time for a "yes, but" so I respond, "Yes, but ... it can make you very, very sick."

Already chomping ice pellets, they ignore me. But perhaps their attraction to ice pellets is my fault anyway. When Jack was a baby he didn't know what sugar was because he never got a taste of it. And I mean never. The closest he got to a sugary snack was a piece of fruit. So when he deserved a treat I gave him an extra-special, low-calorie, fat-free, sugar-free, super-healthy treat straight from our freezer: an ice cube. I would smash up the cube and give him little pieces and he *loved* it. He was in heaven. I was the greatest Mom on earth. Unfortunately, between two grandmas who love to spoil and the birthday-industrial complex, his sugar innocence was corrupted and ice was no longer effective. Just imagine what we could do to childhood obesity if we raised our kids on ice instead of sugar.

As I'm musing about how it all went wrong for us, a little boy about Emmie's age wanders over and starts eating ice as well. His mother is absent-mindedly shoveling raw kale into a container when she shrieks and drops the container on the stainless steel salad bar counter.

"No!" she yells. "No! Connor! Yucky! No!"

She grabs him by the arm and makes Connor spit the ice into her hand. She swings around wildly, dragging Connor back to her cart. Pointing at my kids, who are treating this like a Vegas buffet, he whines, "But they're doing it."

The mother gives me what I can only describe as a look of utter confusion tinged with pity and says, "I don't know why their mommy is letting them do that, but they are going to get very sick."

Listen, awesome mom, I get it. If I saw a bunch of hoodlum children eating ice out of the display case at Whole Foods I would be judging the shit out of that mother for certain. But I would at least be judging her *silently*. Well silently to her face and then publically all over social media. Connor casts a mournful look back at the illicit tub of ice as his mother leads him by the arm to the register. Enjoy your organic kale, lady, I hope it has cow poop on it.

I am dry-heaving at the sight of the continued ice consumption when the inevitable throwing of ice begins. This is actually far more preferable to ingesting the E. coli that is lying suspended in the frozen water, but presents its own set of challenges. Handfuls of ice are strewn about and Emmie is screaming because Jack is smushing ice down the back of her shirt. Emmie spins toward a case holding plastic silverware, napkins and straws and wields a straw as a weapon.

"Hi-ya!" she yells, drawing it like a sword. Not to be outdone, Maeve grabs her own straw and takes up an offensive stance. Jack grabs the straw out of Maeve's hands, causing her to shriek so loudly, no sound discernible to a human ear is emitted. Her face turns red as she turns on him, kicking wildly with her little pink Keens. She needs to learn to protect her sword hand if she's ever going to stand a chance. Jack and Emmie are now lunging and parrying in the frozen foods aisle like they are fighting to the death and Maeve is lying on the floor screaming about her lost straw. I fear for my sanity more than anyone's well-being at this point.

Normally I would have put a halt to this insanity before the first ice cube touched anyone's lips, but now I've stood here allowing this to deteriorate into a ridiculous spectacle. I pinch myself to ensure I'm not dreaming. How the hell did I get here? When I thought about this project in the abstract before I started, it was in terms of the kids asking *for* things. Can I have a sucker? Can I stay up late? Can I fly to Toronto? I never thought about the discipline aspect. It's pretty much impossible to stop any sort of undesirable behavior without saying no. And this is why my children are literally trying to poke someone's eye out in the Whole Foods frozen vegetable section. At least we'll be able to quickly ice down any wounds.

"Pizza's ready!" I yell, instantly bringing the straw fight to a standstill.

That was unusually effective. Three pairs of feet run over to the pizza counter and start hopping around impatiently. I grab the pizza box, place it in the cart and lead them to the checkout like a pied piper. After we pay for the groceries and the pizza in the cart, I lead them to the car with running commentary.

"I just can't believe the behavior in there," I say. "It just boggles my mind. What would possess you to sword-fight with straws? I expect better." My words fall on deaf ears and I wish for once it was closer to Christmas so I could threaten them with Santa. I love parenting in December – one word silences all whining, paralyzes all kicking feet and speeds up all complained-about tasks. But alas, it is not December and I have nothing in my arsenal right now. "I just need you to try harder. Can everyone please just try harder to listen and be good?"

"You know what would make us good?" Jack remarks. "Ice cream!"

"Yeah, ice cream! Mommy can we have ice cream?" Emmie chimes in.

"I want banilla!" Maeve screams.

So that's how we come to be eating ice cream, as an appetizer to our pizza dinner, after some of the most reprehensible grocery store behavior I have ever witnessed. Hopefully they're too young to realize they are being rewarded for bad behavior. At this point, they can't even connect consequences to actions that happened two minutes prior, so I think we're not doing any long-term damage. Regular Mommy would have seen timeouts doled out at the actual grocery store and angry lectures administered on the way home, but Yes Mommy is handing out ice cream cones at the McDonald's drive-thru. What is this world coming to?

CHAPTER NINE
ALL TATTED UP WITH NOWHERE TO GO

When I was growing up my father forbade my sister and I from writing on our hands. If he saw marker or ballpoint ink on our skin, he went ballistic and tried to tell us we could get ink poisoning through our skin. He sufficiently scared the hell out of me enough that I never did it. My friends would cover their hands in rainbows of ink with things like "I love Peter," "Bon Jovi 4 Ever" and smiley faces and I would sadly stare at the back of my freckled, blank skin.

Back in my single days, I once refused to give a guy my number because he was going to write it on his hand. I couldn't be responsible for a slow death by ink. He's probably a vice president at Google right now and I missed out on millions because of my fear of poisoning. Although I'm rich with love and wouldn't trade Josh for all the Google stock in the world! Josh, however, says he would definitely trade me for Google stock and then buy me back. He's very practical.

After growing up in such an environment, one can imagine an actual tattoo was out of the question. My skin remains as fresh as the day I was born, but apparently, my sister thought the "no ink" rule was optional because she got herself a tat when she was a senior in high school.

"Hey, wanna see something? You can't tell Mom and Dad," she said to me one winter afternoon when I was visiting my parents' house.

"Sure – oh my god, what the hell is that?" I yelled, my eyes bugging out of my head. She had lifted the back of her sweatshirt to reveal a stylized black sun on her lower back, just below the waistband of her jeans.

"Shhhhh! They'll hear you," Beth hissed, quickly putting her sweatshirt back in place.

"I can't even believe you did that," I shrieked. "Mom and Dad are going to completely freak out on you."

"No, Mom and Dad are going to do nothing because they're not going to know."

"Not know? That thing is so big you can practically see it from space. You're insane. The ink has gone to your brain and you have brain damage. That's the only explanation for why you've done this and why you think Mom and Dad won't find out."

"They won't. When do they ever see my midriff? You're being ridiculous."

"No, you're being ridiculous. Hello, swimsuit? That thing that completely exposes your lower back? That you wear all summer long? Good luck with that."

"I can wear a one-piece," Beth replied coolly. "I'm not worried. Now keep your mouth shut."

But of course, I couldn't keep my mouth shut. My parents knew within a week. But in typical youngest-child fashion, they never said a word about it to her and acted as if it never happened. If I had a tat in high school, I would have been grounded for the rest of my life. She gets a tramp stamp and nobody says a word. Of course.

So when my own kids started bringing home birthday goody bags containing waterproof tattoos, I got a little twitchy. They'd ask why the "stickers" didn't work and I would innocently say I had no idea and throw them away.

With three kids in the house, we're regulars on the birthday party circuit. Chuck E. Cheese's, Little Gym, My Gym, Lucky Strike, Pump It Up, Jump Zone, Windy City Field House, Lil Kickers – you name it, we've partied there. The kids run around like crazy people, adults corral them to picnic tables for pizza and Costco cake and then release them back to their parents full of sugar with goody bags grasped in their sticky little hands. We conveniently "lost" the tattoos on the way home, and no one was the wiser.

At the conclusion of this weekend's latest preschool rave, Emmie waltzes out to the car with a gleeful look on her face.

"Mommy! Look, we got tattoos!" she says with so much excitement one might think she had been given her own car. I peek into the bag and see that yes, they were given a lot of tattoos. I'll be sure to thank that mother the next time I see her by offering my children chocolate ice cream right in front of hers. At breakfast time.

"That's super," I say, reaching for the bag. Emmie whips her body around so I can't get my hands on it and darts past me to the car door, where she climbs into the third row and buckles herself in. Please know this child has never quickly buckled herself in for any reason, including under threat of adoption. But now that she knows I can't reach her back there, she thinks she's Usain Bolt in the hundred-meter dash. She knows my tactics too well by now.

But because there are three children and only one of me, I switch my focus to the other children who are whining about not being invited to the same party (Maeve: hysterically screaming) and acting out because Emmie won't share her loot (Jack: punching his sister repeatedly in the leg). After imposing a peace accord, I forget all about the goody bag and the offending items inside. When we arrive home, Emmie asks if she can take the goody bag up to her room and, of course, I have to say yes, yes that sounds perfect. Knock yourself out.

The next morning, I wake up to find the first floor of the house eerily quiet. There's a Disney movie playing to an empty living room littered with discarded granola bar wrappers. I walk past the trail of granola crumbs into the bathroom to shut the light off (why don't my children understand the concept of the on/off switch?) and find a sopping wet hand towel in the sink. The children certainly didn't use it to wipe up a gallon of water that has spilled on the countertop and the floor, however, so why exactly it's sopping wet is a mystery. I sigh and replace it with a dry towel, taking the wet one to the laundry closet.

I follow the faint sound of high-pitched voices to the top of the stairs where I use my mommy superpowers to determine all three kids are playing in the basement. I leave them to their activities for a few minutes while I use the hand vacuum to erase the granola brick road on the rug and then make scrambled eggs and toast.

"Guys, breakfast is ready," I yell downstairs. I know they've heard me, but I sense no movement at all. The only sound is the plinking of plastic LEGOs being discarded in a bucket in the search for a certain color and shape.

"Breakfast is ready," I yell again. Still nothing.

"If you don't come up right now, I will eat all your eggs myself," I say and that does the trick. I hear stampeding feet behind me on the stairs as I open the refrigerator and grab the gallon of milk. I close the door and notice I really need to use the stainless cleaner more often. The *CSI* people could identify a print here using nothing but the naked eye. As I turn around, I collide with Maeve, who is standing as close as humanly possible to my legs. She smiles at me and announces, "I have a tattoo, Mommy!"

She thrusts her arm at me and she's right, she has a tattoo of a butterfly on her arm. And not just one, she has four. Rainbows, butterflies, unicorns and bumblebees now cover her perfect, creamy skin. Considering her arm is about as big as a paper towel roll, the tats take up a pretty large piece of real estate. I grit my teeth. She proudly shows me her other arm, which is also covered in tattoos. My three-year-old has a sleeve grown bikers would be proud of.

"Wow, Maeve, that's ... something," I say, choosing my words carefully. "How did you get all those tattoos on yourself?"

"Emmie helped me!" Maeve says proudly, skirting around me to grab her plate off the counter.

"Be care— ! You're going to—" and with that, she drops the plate of eggs and toast on the hardwood floor and immediately starts hysterically screaming. Of course the toast lands mixed-berry-jelly side down and the eggs are scattered in a two-foot radius. Even more awesome? Those were the last of the eggs, so I can't make her more. I try to calm her down while I grab a paper towel to wipe up the jelly, while Jack is helpfully mashing the eggs into the floor while he walks through the chaos to grab his own plate. Seriously?

"Maeve, Maevie, it's fine," I sooth while scooping eggs into my hand. "It's no big deal. See? I cleaned it up."

"I wanted to carry it!" she cries. "I wanted to do it!"

"You did carry it and you dropped it," Jack helpfully points out from the dining room table.

"No I didn't!" Maeve screams. I'm quite sure they heard her three blocks down at the local Starbucks, which is where I would really rather be right now.

"Listen, it's fine," I tell her. "No big deal. We'll make you something else."

"But I want eggs," she howls.

"We don't have more eggs. I have to go to the store to buy some. Jack, would you please give Maeve some of your eggs?"

"No," he says matter of factly, scooping forkfuls of scrambled eggs into his mouth with alarming speed and even more alarming lack of accuracy. "I'm really hungry and I'm not sharing. Give her some of Emmie's." There are enough egg scraps on the placemat around his plate and on the floor beneath where he is sitting to feed every child in this house, but even I wouldn't stoop so low as to scrape the remnants of his eggs off the table and onto Maeve's plate.

"Thanks for being so helpful," I say. "I hope you never need something from your sister – like a kidney – because I will remind her of this very moment when you refused to share your scrambled eggs. And then you'll have to ask Emmie for one of her kidneys, but because you punch her in them all the time, they probably won't even work anymore by then and you will be one very sad dialysis patient, all because you weren't nice to your sisters."

He stares at me. "What's dialysis?"

Oh never mind. Maeve is still sobbing in the kitchen when I kneel down and look her in the eyes.

"Maevie, I'm sorry your eggs fell on the floor and trust me, I'm even sorrier that I don't have more to give you," I say in my very nicest mommy voice. "But you can have anything else you want."

She stops crying. "Pizza?"

If there's one thing we always have on hand, it's leftover pizza. Josh has a blind-spot when it comes to pizza estimates. If we need a medium, he always orders a large. He once ordered eight Chicago-style pizzas (that's deep-dish with cheese in the middle and sauce on the top, for those not in the know) for ten people at a birthday party. His excuse is that we can always eat the leftovers, so my freezer is filled with Ziploc bags full of pizza slices from different places all over the north side of Chicago. For once, I am thankful for his lack of successful estimation as I pull a bag of thin-crust Lou Malnati's from the freezer drawer. I pop it in the microwave and watch as Maeve picks pieces of egg off the floor and sticks them in her mouth. The floors were just mopped yesterday, it's probably fine. And besides, if it means she stops screaming, I'm fine with it.

After putting a piece of piping hot pizza pie on her orange plastic plate, I admonish her to blow on it because it's really hot and carry it to the table myself. I'm not going through this nonsense again. I turn back into the kitchen and do a double-take when I see Emmie at the top of the basement staircase. Emmie has tattoos of ladybugs on both cheeks and her forehead. My mouth hangs open for a second before I snap out of it and find my voice.

"Emily! What on earth have you done?" I say.

"What?" she asks, genuinely unconcerned.

I march her into the bathroom so she can see her reflection. "This," I say, pointing to her cheeks.

"Oh, those are tattoos, Mommy!" she says excitedly.

You're kidding me. I thought a two-inch-long mutant ladybug landed on your face.

"Why? Are? They? On? Your? Face?" I ask, spitting each word out staccato.

"I like them there. I want breakfast."

She slithers out of my grip and grabs her own plate off the counter, taking it to the dining room.

"Hey, why does Maeve get pizza for breakfast?" Emmie whines. "These eggs are yucky. They're cold. I want pizza. Can I have pizza?"

"Yeah, I want pizza, too," Jack whines.

I take a deep breath. Is it too early for a drink? Some bars make Bloody Marys with bacon in them, surely that's considered a breakfast food. "Coming right up!" I say with fake cheerfulness.

I plunk down two more plates of pizza and Jack and Emmie smile with delight. Maeve starts making faces with the pizza crust and the two big kids howl with laughter, then start in on their own edible art, each trying to be more ridiculous. When Emmie puts a piece of pizza upside down on top of her hair, I literally bite my tongue to stop myself from saying, "stop it right now." I'm thinking *no no no no no nooooooo* but keeping my face impassive. I think my blood pressure has just shot up fifty points as I try to hold it in. The old mommy would have sent everyone to timeout by now; the new mommy is hiding in the kitchen, digging her fingernails into her palms. Emmie has oregano in the part of her hair when I finally come back into the room, but still I say nothing. Maeve is laughing so hard she almost falls backwards off the bench seat and I figure stitches in the noggin aren't part of the Yes Mommy plan, so I tell them breakfast is over.

"Dis was da best bwekfist ever!" Maeve yells. Indeed.

"Yeah, Mommy, how come we've never had pizza for breakfast before?" Jack asks.

Because you're not in college yet?

Oregano in her hair is the least of my problems, however, as I stare at Emmie's cheeks. At least her bangs conceal the rainbow tattoo on her forehead. I hustle them all upstairs to get ready for camp and choose to ignore the alarming arthropods marring her smooth cheeks. There's nothing I can do about it now.

A few hours later, I get a call from her camp director.

"Hi, Mrs. Sprenger? I wanted to let you know about a situation that came up today with Emmie," she said.

"Is she okay?" I ask worriedly. I envision a scraped knee, a broken arm, tears.

"Oh, she's fine," she says with seriousness. "But she apparently pulled down her skirt to show the other girls her tattoo."

"Why would she do that? The tattoos on her cheeks are visible from space. I'm sure you saw them. I swear to you, I had no idea what she was up to." Lovely, now I am admitting lax parental supervision to another adult. What a stellar day this is shaping up to be.

"Umm, not those cheeks, Mrs. Sprenger. She showed them a tattoo on her butt."

"Emmie most certainly doesn't have a tattoo on her butt," I say indignantly.

"Well, she actually does. It's Hello Kitty. Or so I hear from the girls in her group. They now all want Hello Kitty tattoos on their butts. We had to explain to them why this isn't appropriate."

I am so embarrassed I want to crawl in a hole. My daughter is mooning her groupmates and encouraging them to tattoo their asses. It's all gone off the rails. I assure the woman I will speak to Emmie when she gets home and she thanks me for my time. When I pick her up, I don't even have to say a word before Emmie flings herself at me sobbing.

"I'm sorry, I'm sorry," she sobs. "I put a tattoo on my butt and I showed it to everyone and I got in trouble."

I smooth her hair and crouch down to look her in the face. I wipe the tears away from the ladybugs and tuck stray strands of blonde hair behind her ears. She looks so pathetic I can't even get upset. I hug her and tell her we'll talk about it later. She sniffles and holds my hand on the way home as Jack retells the now infamous story about Emmie's butt tattoo. "Mommy! Everybody knows! I told her she was going to be in so much trouble." Thanks for supporting your sister, big man.

"She's not in trouble," I say. "But let's just all think about this the next time we get a tattoo. Tattoos are for our hands or our arms. One at a time. Not for faces or legs – or butts."

Maeve stops and pulls up her pink tanktop in the middle of the sidewalk and yells, "And not for belly buttons!" Sure as shit, she has a flower tattoo around her belly button.

"I helped her put it there," Emmie says in a whisper. She lifts up her own shirt to reveal a matching flower tattoo.

That's the last time I allow a birthday goody bag in the house, hand to god. I don't care how much the kids whine and complain.

CHAPTER TEN
PARENTING BY BRIBERY

I lean back on the couch, surveying the damage of the day. There are four dolls lined up sweetly under a blanket in the corner near the stairs, a Magnadoodle with some half-erased math equations is discarded near the edge of the rug, an iPad and an iPod Touch are face-down on the chair, and there are enough LEGO pieces spread out in the middle of the rug to build a full-scale reproduction of the White House. I see dress-up dresses in pink poufy heaps with plastic high-heeled slippers peeking out from under them. Random crayons and a coloring book, a play cash register and a puzzle – completed triumphantly and later destroyed by a marauding sibling – are strewn about. It looks like a toy store threw up in my living room. I don't even want to know what the basement playroom looks like.

Jack, Emmie and Maeve are upstairs and haven't required intervention for several minutes, which means they're plotting a hostile coup. I can hear their laughter over the monitor in Maeve's room and then I hear Jack. "Okay, this is the roller coaster," he says. "Maeve you get in first and then Emmie, you get in last. Okay. Welcome to Six Flags Chicago. Please hold on at all times and keep your hands inside the coaster."

I hear a commotion involving running and pounding and screaming that shakes the whole house and gets increasingly louder and closer to me. I walk to the top of the stairs to find Jack pushing the two girls in a green plastic laundry basket. Maeve is wearing a glittery blue Cinderella dress and a Spiderman mask, which covers her entire face. Emmie is wearing an old lilac-colored bridesmaid dress of mine, a headband that looks like a snowflake and Barbie sunglasses. Jack runs the length of the hall pushing the basket and the girls scream with delight. When they take the curve into Emmie's room, the basket hits the corner of the doorway and the girls are thrown forward, Emmie hitting her face on the back of Maeve's head. Both girls immediately start crying and Jack protests it was an accident.

"Sorry, but the park has mandated we shut this ride down and inspect it for mechanical defects," I say, hugging Emmie and rubbing the back of Maeve's noggin. "I know you didn't do it on purpose. While we wait for the Occupational Safety and Health Administration findings, it's time to clean up downstairs."

Howls of protest meet this pronouncement. Emmie falls on the floor and curls up in a ball while Maeve runs to her room and hides in the closet. Jack ignores me completely and tries to grab the laundry basket out of my hands. "Guys, downstairs, now," I say.

Emmie army-crawls and rolls dramatically toward the stairs, the entire time emitting a noise that is half human and half wounded squirrel. Jack steps on her as he walks by, acting surprised when she yells out and kicks him in the leg. I honestly don't think he is capable of keeping his hands off of her for more than thirty consecutive seconds. When they were much younger, I was concerned by his tendency toward extreme and constant violence. I even mentioned it to my friend, Leah, over dinner once.

"I never had a brother, I have no idea if just walking up to someone and belting them in the back of the head for no reason reveals a tendency towards sadistic behavior," I moaned. "The worst thing I ever did to my sister was dump a container of Sunny Delight over her head when she wouldn't give me the remote control."

"Oh, it's totally normal," she said, waving her hand. "My brother used to beat the heck out of me all the time when we were growing up. See this? He broke my finger once and I had to miss a gymnastics meet because of it. But I was so scared of what my parents would do to him that I never told on him."

"Leah, that's not normal, that's abuse."

"Nah, it was fine. And look how close we are now!"

I gesture to the floor of the living room and tell the kids it all needs to be cleaned up before bedtime. And the longer they take, the less time they will have to read books. Howls of protest greet my announcement. I love that my kids are actually upset when they lose reading time – makes my bookworm heart happy. Emmie slithers down the steps instead of walking and crawls over to the couch, where I have planted myself. I didn't take any of these toys out and I am certainly not putting any of them away. Unless putting them away involves a garbage bag and the Salvation Army drop-off truck.

"No, I am *not* cleaning up," Emmie says, crossing her arms and taking a stance.

And here is the beauty of this experiment, something I learned very early on. "Oh yes, you are!"

When the kids say no, I am absolutely empowered to say yes. It's genius.

"No!" she says, digging in.

"Yes," I sing. "Yes yes yes yes yes."

"Mommy! Stop saying yes!"

Oh, Emily, you have no idea how much I would like to do exactly that.

"How many toys do we have to pick up?" Jack asks.

"Umm, all of them?" I say.

"But I didn't play with this stuff!"

"And I didn't wear all the clothes in the laundry, but I still have to wash them all and fold them all and put them all away."

Emmie has quietly picked up a crayon and is coloring Snow White. I have never seen Snow White in an orange dress, but that doesn't mean it couldn't happen. "Emmie! Come on! You need to clean up!" I grab the crayon out of her hand and close the coloring book.

"Hey! No! I am coloring!" she yells at me.

"You *were* coloring, *now* you are cleaning," I respond coolly.

This sets her off into a fresh round of crying. Jack is sitting in the middle of the floor constructing something with the LEGOs instead of cleaning them up. I look skyward and count to ten silently. When I am done, Jack looks at me. "What are you doing?" he asks suspiciously.

"Thinking about how happy I am going to be when the living room is cleaned up," I respond. I silently add, "*in fifteen years when you are all at college.*"

"Mommy, if we clean up can we have ice cream?" he asks suddenly.

"Yes, as a matter of fact, you can," I say.

Emmie stops her whining and immediately starts throwing toys in the toy box. Babies are flying through the air, doll clothes flung into bins. Maeve comes to the top of the steps and says, "Ice cream?" The child can't hear me when I am sitting right next to her on the couch and ask her to put on her shoes, but she heard the words "ice cream" from two floors and five rooms away through a closed door.

"Yep, anyone who cleans up gets ice cream," I confirm.

Maeve starts grabbing handfuls of LEGOs and throwing them in the bin. It's a blur of primary colors as she runs back and forth from one side of the rug to the other. Jack is stacking books on the shelf like he's a librarian, although his Dewey Decimal System knowledge could use an update. Minutes later, the room is spotless and the children look wildly around for any stray items. Maeve sees a tiny Mickey Mouse squinkie and pounces on it, lest this half-inch tall rubber nubbin be the cause of ice cream denial.

I must admit, bribery is one of my favorite forms of parenting. It requires minimal nagging on my part and maximum efficiency on theirs. It's beautiful. But you can't go around bribing your children all the time, they'll just grow up expecting to be paid for their efforts and hard work. Wait, that's not right. Maybe I'm on to something here.

"Can we have ice cream now?" they ask. Let's do this.

I open the freezer and they each choose a different flavor. Yes, we have several flavors on hand. One can never have too many choices when it comes to ice cream. Plus, with all the bribery parenting up in here, we need fully-stocked provisions.

Maeve says she wants vanilla, so I oblige her, while Jack asks if he can scoop his own. Hey, knock yourself out. Emmie asks if she can have as much as she wants and I tell her yes. Pushing the envelope, she says, "I want to eat it out of the container."

I hesitate. "Okay, here you go," I say, handing over a spoon. Her eyes light up and she claps her hands. "Actually, I want *that* ice cream." She points to the holy grail of the freezer, my container of high-end Talenti caramel-cookie-crunch gelato. This is the ice cream I hide under the frozen broccoli in the back of the freezer and consume only once the children are in bed and I know they are asleep. At six bucks a pint, it's my precious ice cream and I go a little Gollum and *Lord of the Rings* on anyone who dares come near it. Josh once accused me of loving the gelato more than him. It was a tense few minutes.

I swallow my cry of "no" and silently unscrew the top and hand her the pint. She takes it to the dining room table where she starts hacking indiscriminately at it. Doesn't she know you lovingly scrape spoonfuls off the top in equal portions? You don't stab at it, making craters where the cookie pieces used to be. You slide the spoon along, leveling the surface and enjoying the feel of the cold cream and the silky caramel juxtaposed with the crunch of random cookie pieces. She is relishing the ice cream, all right, but it's like watching a death-metal show instead of an opera. I have to turn away because I can't bear to watch.

Jack finally looks up from his own dessert and instantly asks why Emmie is eating out of the container. I have no response and when he asks if he can do it, too, I walk into the kitchen, open the freezer and wordlessly hand him the half-gallon container of the mint chocolate chip. Maeve gets in on the action after filing her own lawsuit alleging unfair ice cream consumption practices, although she quickly tires of the work that goes into scooping her own ice cream and announces she's done.

Josh wanders in to the kitchen and gapes at the children, who are happily – and silently – spooning ice cream straight from the container. He turns slowly to look at me and I pretend to inspect my manicure. Well, actually, what would be a manicure if I got them. Instead I stare at my ragged cuticles and unfiled nailtips of varying lengths and think about how I really should take better care of them.

"Care to explain this?" he asks.

"Nope," I respond.

"Looks like we're raising a bunch of animals around here," Josh says.

"Why even give them spoons? Just let them eat out of the container with their mouths like some ice-cream-eating contest."

"Daddy! Daddy! Do you want some ice cream?" Emmie asks excitedly.

"No, thanks," Josh says. "Especially not after you've all eaten out of the container."

He goes to the fridge and rummages around. "Hey, do we have any Canadian bacon?" he asks.

"No, no we do not have any Canadian bacon, dear," I say sweetly. "We seem to be fresh out."

"Huh. That's weird. Can you add it to the store list, please?"

I grit my teeth and nod. He tells Emmie that on second thought, he will have some ice cream. By this time the kids have had enough and drift away from the table, abandoning their containers. I survey the damage and wince when I see my poor Talenti container, looking like a mine field, divots where cookies once lay, giant spoon-sized holes in the landscape. Josh picks it up and starts eating it.

"Hey, that's mine!" I say.

"No, it's actually Emmie's and she offered it to me," he says.

"Don't be ridiculous. It's mine."

"I'm ridiculous? I didn't just give my child carte blanche with a container of ice cream and a spoon. Let's reassess our definitions of ridiculous here."

"Well, they did clean up the living room."

"I led six meetings today, answered two hundred emails and drafted a proposal that could lead to a million dollars in business for my company. You don't see anyone offering me the keys to a Ben & Jerry's shop. Perhaps they should have cleaned up the toys *because they were the ones who took them out.*"

"You parent your way, I'll parent mine."

"That's pretty much standard operating procedure around here."

"Yeah, well guess what? All the toys were cleaned up in record time and nobody was yelling or threatening to throw away all the toys. For once, they cleaned up without any directions or screaming on my part."

"Of course they cleaned up, you bribed them."

"You give them allowance based on the chores they do, how is this any different? I just cut out the middle man and instead of making them pay me my own money back for the ice cream, I handed them the cold deliciousness myself."

I smugly walk away, although Josh gets the final word in the form of finishing every last bite of my ice cream. This yes thing is working out pretty well. My house is clean, my kids are happy and my freezer has more space. It's a win-win for everyone.

CHAPTER ELEVEN
IT'S ALL FUN AND GAMES
UNTIL IT'S YES *WIFE* TIME

"Will you rub my back?" Josh asks one night while I'm in bed reading.

"No," I say without even looking up from my iPad. "That's why people go to massage school. Make an appointment with one of them."

"That is such bullshit," he says. "You can't say no the kids, but you can say it whenever you feel like it to me."

"That's the beauty of marriage – you're legally obligated to be as miserable as I am. It's in the vows. For richer, for poorer, sickness, health, blah, blah, blah."

"Did you just blah-blah-blah our marriage vows? Because there's plenty of room for interpretation in several areas if that's how we're going to roll."

"Listen, the kids are all over me all day long. *Mommy, I want milk. Mommy, I want to watch a video. Mommy, I want to sit on your lap. Mommy, I want to play beauty shop and tie your hair in knots that need to be cut out.* I just want to sit here quietly and read my book."

"So you don't want to have sex then?"

I don't even acknowledge the comment and keep reading.

"How about next month instead of Yes Mommy you do Yes Wife?" Josh asks.

"There is nothing in my life I'd rather do less than Yes Wife. You know what we could do instead? No Wife. How about that? How does that work for you?"

"Where have you been? I already have No Wife. I've lived with her for almost ten years now. She's a total drag."

I turn the virtual page with a swipe of my finger and look up at his smirking face. *Yes Wife* would have to be shelved in the fiction section because we all know that would never really happen. And it would totally be a book written by a dude.

"Whatever. If I did Yes Wife, you'd make me your sex slave or something ridiculous like that. I wouldn't be able to leave the bedroom and nothing would ever get done around here."

"You think I would ask to have sex with *you* if you were Yes Wife? I already get that with a snap of my fingers. It's like bringing sand to the beach." I snort in response and he continues. "Give me some credit here. I think I'd be a little more creative. Well, a lot more creative."

"Like what?"

"I don't know, maybe a three-way?"

I close the iPad cover and laugh hysterically. I wipe tears from my eyes before replying. "Really? Well, you would need one more to make that happen. Who exactly do you think is going be into that?"

"One more? You mean two more," he says with authority.

"Two more? Check your addition. You, me, and someone who you hope is out there, but likely doesn't exist, makes three."

"What makes you think I'd invite you to my three-way?"

"That's not very nice."

"Unless you're a smoking hot model or a movie star, you're not invited to my three-way. I only get one chance at this and that's the minimum requirement. I'm like a roller coaster – instead of 'must be this tall to ride this coaster' it's 'must be smoking hot model or movie star to ride this coaster.'"

I can't hide my bemused smile. This is so ridiculous I can't even believe we're discussing it. But because I like nothing more than to coax ridiculous material from my life, I continue on with this line of discussion. "And who exactly is going to want to ride such a mediocre coaster?"

"That was a low blow. I'm like the Top Thrill Dragster coaster at Cedar Point. It's the tallest, fastest, steepest coaster in the world."

"Let me guess, and over in sixty seconds?" I interrupt with peals of laughter.

"That's enough out of you. Bottom line, you're not invited."

"And who exactly is invited to take part in this thrill ride?"

"I hear Canadian women love Americans."

Oh for the love of god. I know a few Canadian women and they've never mentioned their patriotic duty involving threesomes with American men. "Oh really, how would that work exactly? Is there some stop right over the border where you can get a pair of hockey skates sharpened, exchange your American dollars for Canadian loonies and peruse a lineup of women who are just waiting to fulfill all your wildest fantasies?"

"I would just walk into a bar in Canada and women would get the American vibe from me. All I'd have to do is wave two fingers above my head and the hot Canadian women would flock to me asking – no, *begging* – for a three-way with me."

"Do you actually hear yourself? Do the words coming out of your mouth sound normal to you? Because they sound insane to me. You are not having a threesome with anyone – Canadian or otherwise. Got it? I'm going to bed. Go do whatever it is that you do with your little video games until two in the morning and leave me alone. And if I look in your browser history and find anything about Canadian three-ways, I swear to god, I will change the Internet password and not tell you."

Josh sighs and goes downstairs. Maybe I'll throw him a bone and do twenty-four hours of yes. And like the kids, I'm not going to tell him about the little experiment, I'll just man up and get it done for a day. How bad can it be? Clearly, I won't be having any threesomes, but a little positivity never hurt anyone.

The next morning when Maeve calls for us at the ungodly hour of five-thirty, Josh moans and says, "Your turn." Rather than argue about whose turn it is to get up, and I know damn well that it's definitely his day, I get out of bed and escort her downstairs. This is a big one as I have a mental calendar dating back seven years and I can tell you exactly which days were Josh's and which were mine. The last Tuesday in January 2009? Mine. June 10, 2007? Josh. The officiant at your wedding should really tell you about this running mental tally when you sign the license. Dishes, laundry, getting up with the baby, taking the wheel on roadtrips, which relatives you visited for Thanksgiving – it all adds up. Anyone who says she doesn't keep score is lying – it just means she's winning.

The other kids eventually trail downstairs and I make breakfast, letting Josh sleep in. Normally I would be making as much noise as possible, going in and out of the bedroom to get dressed, letting the kids play upstairs and generally being a bitch about him sleeping late. But today he emerges from the bedroom around ten, looking confused.

"Why'd you let me sleep in?" he asks suspiciously.

"Because I love you," I say, kissing him on his stubbly cheek.

"Liar," he says. "I'm taking a shower."

This would normally be the time where I snippily tell him that he slept until ten and it's my turn to sneak away from the children for a bit, but instead I smile and tell him to go ahead. Jack asks if we can go to the park and while I would much rather sit on the couch and do nothing, I smile and say yes. I get dressed, throwing on a red sundress and brown flip-flops and grab my keys. The kids are already wearing their sandals and scramble toward the front door. A blast of hot, humid air hits me in the face and I take a shallow breath. My hair immediately starts to curl and I curse the Midwestern humidity for what's sure to be another less-than-stellar hair day.

The kids and I walk the two blocks to the park and find it strangely empty for a weekend mid-morning. The splashpad portion of the park has a few kids in it, but it too is unusually quiet. The kids take off running toward the swings and immediately beg me to push them. I give everyone a few pushes and step back into the shade, wondering if it's too soon to give the five-minute warning that we're leaving. Sweat is running down the backs of my legs and I'm really regretting this little outing right now. Jack's cheeks are bright, splotchy red and he's complaining he needs a drink of water because it's so hot. I hear him whine, "Can we go in the water?"

I haven't brought swimsuits for anyone, but the girls take up the battle call. "Yeah, can we Mommy?"

Of course we can! And the three kids are sopping wet in their clothes in thirty seconds flat. Jack at least takes his shirt off, and Emmie and Maeve have on little tank tops and skorts, so it's not a big deal. I even put my feet in the water and marvel at how much cooler I feel. I find a bench in the shade and sit down, pulling my phone out to check my e-mail. Gap, junk, junk, Nigerian bank scam! I immediately send both my personal checking account information as well as my social security number to a man I have never met before because I know he will absolutely come through on his end and route the money back to me next week.

As I am scrolling through my Twitter feed, I hear a commotion in front of me. There's some general screaming and yelling, which I am adept at ignoring. I'm a professional when it comes to pretending not to notice when my children are using their outside voices, and since we're actually outside, I figure it can't be that much of a problem. I quickly glance up and see my three children hurling buckets of water at each other. They're sopping wet, but they're having a grand time. The other five moms in the fenced-in area are giving my kids dirty looks and I wonder if I could easily slink out now before they figure out I'm the mom of the crazy coalition. Jack refills a red bucket and launches it at Emmie and misses, which is unfortunate for the little boy behind Emmie, because he takes it full in the face. Oops.

The little boy starts to cry and I spring off the bench and ask if he's okay. He sobs, pointing at Jack and the bucket. Jack is clearly sorry, I see it in his face, and he comes over to apologize to the boy without being asked. The boy's mom is at his side by now, kneeling down and hugging him, murmuring in his ear. She stands up and whirls around.

"Why don't you control your kids?" she hisses.

Whoa. I get it, your child was wronged. But let's be clear: we're in a water park, surrounded by cascading water and your kid's already soaked to the skin. It was an unfortunate situation for which I am more than ready to apologize. But I don't think we need to get personal.

"I'm sorry," I say quickly. "They were just playing and my daughter ducked at the right time. Well, I guess the wrong time for your son. But again, I'm really sorry."

"Your kids have been running around terrorizing the other kids while you've been busy on your phone over there," she says caustically. Oh momma, now it's on. "They're not even wearing swimming suits."

"Well, we weren't planning to go in the water," I start. "But I can't say … " I trail off and stop mid-sentence. Why the hell do I need to explain myself to sanctimommy over here? "You know what, I said I was sorry. It won't happen again."

As I turn to walk away, Emmie launches a bucket of water – straight at me. I am drenched from the middle of my head through my torso. Sanctimommy's mouth hangs open and I turn on my heel. I push the hair out of my face and squelch the urge to scream, "Stop!" and see Emmie's face. She doesn't know if she should laugh or run away, she's so freaked out. And for once in my life, instead of yelling, I start laughing. So Emmie starts laughing in response and runs away. I grab a bucket, hold it under the cascading water and sneak up behind Emmie, drenching her. Maeve begs, "Do it to me, Mommy! Do it to me!" So I refill the bucket and chase after her, getting her square in the back. Jack sneaks up behind me and throws it all over the bottom of my dress, which is now sticking to me in the all the wrong places. The four of us chase each other around for a few minutes and the other moms look at me like I'm crazy. Trust me, if I was watching some other mom do this, I would be looking at her the exact same way.

Yes Mommy is certainly having more fun than my old self, but she's not making any friends. Which is fine, because I already have all the mom friends I need. They're just not at the park right now to witness me losing my mind and running around in a soaking wet sundress, which is a good thing.

I round the kids up and tell them it's time to head home for lunch. Sanctimommy is sitting on a bench near the gate chatting with another mom as I walk by, but I say, "By the way, you might want to check your kid – he's over there drinking puddle water like it's going out of style." She gives me a dirty look, but jumps up to grab him and drag him away from the rogue puddle of sludge on the edge of the splashpad.

When we get home, Josh can't stop laughing at me. I ask him politely to get towels for the kids and me while they excitedly jump around and tell him how Mommy had a water fight with them. Apparently it's the most exciting thing I've ever done as a mother, including the time I let them eat ice cream for dinner.

"See? Get your face out of your phone once in a while and look what happens," Josh says. "I always play with them at the park. This would just be a day in the life if it was me."

I bite my tongue and don't say what I'm really thinking, which is, "Stop talking." That would violate the spirit of my twenty-four hours of yes, although it would certainly make me feel better.

"Hey, Matt asked if I want to meet up tonight," Josh says. I love when Josh's single friends ask him to go out on weekends. He travels all week for work, so when he's actually around on Fridays and Saturdays, I expect him to hang out with me. So normally him going out with a friend on a Saturday night would be a huge issue and result in me being bitchy, Josh being annoyed and nobody having a good time the night we're supposed to be hanging out together. Imagine his surprise when I enthusiastically tell him he should go.

He glances at me and grabs his phone to text Matt, before I can change my mind. Afterward, he sits down on the couch and turns on the baseball game. I run upstairs and change into a pair of khaki shorts and a black tank. My wet hair isn't worth salvaging, so I pull it into a high ponytail and go back downstairs and start making lunch. I slap some almond butter and jelly on honey whole-wheat bread for my special snowflakes – they turn their noses up at peanut butter – and peel a couple of carrots before slicing them into sticks. We're so old-school with the food choices we don't even give the kids baby carrots. Those things are drenched in bleach to "clean" them before they're packaged and consumed. So I'm paying an extra buck for organic carrots that are then dunked in bleach? No, thanks anyway. I sling some red grapes on their plates and announce lunch is ready, which sets off the arguing over who gets which plate.

"I want the pink one!" Maeve screams from the stairs. She hasn't even reached the general vicinity of the kitchen and she's already calling dibs on a plate? The rule when I was growing up was you had to be in sight of the item before calling dibs. I remember some knock-down, drag-em-outs with Beth over rights to the front seat on car rides. Ahh, the good old days when seven-year-olds could ride in the front seat and without a booster. My mother would be arrested in this day and age. Maeve runs as fast as her little legs will carry her and slides to a stop in front of the kitchen island, where she opens her mouth and lets out a blood-curdling scream when she sees I have set out the food on identical orange plates with milk in identical green cups. "I want pink," she screams. And I want a kid who doesn't scream about the color of her lunch plate. You get what you get, and you don't get upset – sage advice from the mother of *Pinkalicious*.

I silently turn to the cupboard, take out a pink plate, dump the contents of the orange plate onto it, and hand it to Maeve, who takes it and immediately drops it on the floor. *God give me strength*, I think. I debate the five-second rule in my head, knowing damn well there is no such thing, and figure this is the child who puts rocks in her mouth at the park, surely eating a sandwich and some grapes off the floor (scrubbed somewhat recently) won't kill her. I replace the items and walk it to the table myself. Emmie sidles up behind me and wedges herself between her chair and the table, whining, "Why does Maeve get a pink plate?" I shoot her a look and she stares me down, but hunger wins out and she eventually picks up a carrot and starts eating. And because my children are nothing if not predictable, Jack places his plate down on the table and I do a double-take when I see it is pink. "What? I wanted a pink one," he says through a mouthful of sandwich. I turn on my heel and walk back to the kitchen, grab a pink plate and hand it to Emmie, who lights up and thanks me.

"Wanna make me a panini?" Josh asks hopefully from the living room.

"I would love to make you a panini," I say brightly. "Coming right up!"

"Wait, seriously?" Josh asks.

"Serious as a heart attack."

I get out the panini press and the turkey, cheese, bread and Thousand Island dressing. I lovingly craft a sandwich for my husband, plate it with a handful of Trader Joe's barbecue potato chips and deliver it to him in the living room. He genuinely smiles and thanks me. I go back to make a sandwich for myself and find Maeve standing at the counter, eating the last piece of cheese. "Mommy! I eat cheese!" she says excitedly.

"I see that," I say unexcitedly. "That was the last piece of cheese and now Mommy can't have a sandwich."

"Saw-wy, Mommy," she says. "But you can have annond-butter-jelly!"

The remnants of baby talk and mispronunciations still kill me. I smile and thank her for the suggestion of almond butter and jelly. Josh finishes his sandwich and brings his plate to the kitchen. I wordlessly take it from him and put it in the dishwasher. Josh hugs me and Maeve wiggles her way between our legs. "Daddy, why are you hugging Mommy? Hug me! Hug me!"

Well then.

Later that afternoon, I notice Josh has a browser window open to Kayak.com on his laptop.

"Planning a getaway?" I ask.

"Well, Ian's fortieth birthday trip is coming up fast and I need to make a decision. I'm just checking into flights," Josh says nervously. Our friend, Ian, turns forty this summer and has scheduled a guys-only scuba-diving trip to La Paz, Mexico so he can dive with the whale sharks. I mean doesn't everyone schedule a whale-diving trip for his fortieth? His wife, Heidi, declared it nonsense and wanted no part of swimming with whales as large as a bus, and told him to knock himself out with the guys. Thanks for taking one for the team, *Heidi*, now I'm stuck watching three kids by myself for a weekend. That is, if I even let Josh go. He already takes one stupid "mancation" every year when he goes snowboarding with his friends. Now he wants some bachelor-type party in Mexico, too? Except he picked the exact right time to bring it up, apparently.

"I can use miles and leave Wednesday and come back Saturday," he says. "Everyone else is going for the whole week. I figured this was a nice compromise. Should I book it?"

Every fiber of my being wants to scream, *"No, no you should not book it! You should stay home with the children you don't see because you travel for work all week, jackass."* Instead I smile wanly and give him a thumbs-up. "Go for it," I manage to force out of my mouth.

"Really?" he asks, eyes wide. "Great! Ian's going to be thrilled."

Ian's going to front you the money for a divorce attorney when you get back, too, because I'm going to be so pissed you went to Mexico without me, I think. Josh instantly books the ticket and texts Ian that he's in. There are so many massages in my future, I can't even begin to add them up.

"Well, yeah, I guess, if you want to do that instead of your mancation this year," I respond. It's kind of a roundabout "yes, but." I'm not saying "no" to anything, I'm just saying yes and simply suggesting he continue with the general agreement we have that he is allowed one guy's trip a year. Well, a general agreement that I have, one he hasn't ever actually signed on to.

"Oh no, that's not what I'm saying at all," Josh responds. "Not going on mancation isn't even up for discussion. Do I need to remind you this is the twentieth anniversary of that trip? We haven't even been married ten years and you want me to break a commitment I've had for twenty years?"

"Maybe I missed it, but at some point was there a ceremony where you invited all your friends and family to watch you promise to love your mancation buddies in sickness and in health, until death do you part?"

"No, not yet, but that's something we're seriously considering adding."

"I know this might be a shock to you, but your mancation isn't a marriage. And there's no way it's the twentieth anniversary because you didn't even go on that stupid trip until we had Emmie, and she's only five."

"No, the mancation *started* twenty years ago. I never said it was consecutive."

"Funny how you didn't even mention that trip until we had our second kid and now it's like your damn birthright or something."

"So, bottom line, can I do mancation *and* Ian's birthday or not?"

"N ... " The word starts to slip out, but I bite my tongue and hold it back. "Yes, of course you can, honey. Because I love you soooo much and I want you to be happy." I don't even take a sarcastic tone. I try to appear as genuine as possible, despite the fact I am screaming "no" on the inside.

Josh squints at me and hesitates. "So I can seriously go or are you joking?"

"Yes, you can go Josh." I say, forcing a fake smile.

"Are you feeling okay, because I have to be honest, I wasn't expecting this answer."

"Yes, feeling fantastic. What can I say? I'm feeling quite generous today." Little did I know that last line would come back and bite me right in the ass.

"Generous? Really? Well, I wasn't even planning on bringing this one up at all, but since you're feeling generous today, maybe it's the perfect time. Ed got tickets to the Pearl Jam concert in New York and Niki has to be out of town for work. He asked if I want the other ticket. They're third row, so kind of hard to turn down. Can I go to that too?"

At this point I'm seriously thinking of shutting down this whole thing. Unlike my kids, who when I say "yes" to something I normally wouldn't, might forget about that instance, Josh will not only remember it, but try his damndest to make it the new normal. But I soldier on. "The answer is yes, but there is a high probability of this answer changing if you ask at a different time."

"Does it look like I was born yesterday? I already booked these trips with non-refundable fares while we were talking, making it nearly impossible for you to take any of this back. This ain't my rookie year, you know."

I bite my lip. "Good for you."

Later, after I feed the kids and give them showers while Josh plays *Settlers of Catan* on the Xbox, he casually asks, "What do you want for dinner?"

"Oh, I don't care. What do you want, dear?" I smile at him and twirl my ponytail around my finger.

"Giordano's?" he asks hopefully. In Chicago, we take our pizza seriously and Giordano's is one of the holy trinity along with Lou Malnati's and Gino's East. I haven't eaten commercial pizza, and by commercial pizza I mean Pizza Hut or Domino's, since I've moved here. Why eat cardboard when you can have the best money can buy? But Josh loves Giordano's and I love Lou Malnati's, so we agree to disagree – and eat Lou's. When Josh is out with his friends, they get Giordano's and everyone is happy. For him to ask this means he knows the jig is up. No wonder he made the move on the Mexico trip.

I smack him on the thigh. "You totally think I'm doing Yes Wife, don't you?"

"I totally *know* you're doing Yes Wife," he responds. "Duh. Like you ever let me sit around on weekends and do nothing. I knew the minute you let me sleep in. I just played along so I could get the Mexico and New York trips out of you."

"You're such a jerk! I can't believe you."

"Hey, you're the one who – Hi, I'd like to order a large cheese for pick-up ... " he holds a finger up to shush me. "Yep, that's it. No, thank *you*! So anyway, you're the one who came up with this brilliant idea, not me. See it through, baby."

I sulk on the couch. "You should be happy. I'm amazing."

He kisses me. "Oh, I'm happy, all right. I'm going to Mexico to dive with whale sharks! I'm going to New York to see Pearl Jam! And you're totally right, what an amazing wife I have! I slept in, I'm going on another mancation, I'm eating Giordano's. This is unprecedented. Oh, and I'm going out with Matt tonight! This is epic."

I glare at him and say nothing.

"But honey, let's be clear, this is just everyday life with my Canadian wife. She lets me do whatever I want all the time. You really need to step it up. Oh, and definitely wait up for me tonight. I'm going to make it worth your while."

I wonder if spousal abuse is illegal in Canada?

CHAPTER TWELVE
THE BLOODY COUP

Six months ago Beth called me to ask if we wanted to go on a family vacation in the North Woods of Wisconsin. It would be a re-creation of the trips of our youth, complete with lodging at the very same rustic resort. I hemmed and hawed, but she was persistent. I'm no longer used to roughing it after numerous stays at the St. Regis and Waldorf Astoria properties (thanks to Josh's travel and accumulation of massive quantities of hotel points) and the idea of a cottage with no television, air conditioning or Internet access filled me with dread. If I can't check my Facebook feed every fifteen minutes, I get a little twitchy.

Mostly, I hesitated because I didn't want to subject my extended family to Yes Mommy. We have different viewpoints on raising children and the appropriate level of junk food consumption: I have a zero-tolerance policy; Beth thinks vegetables are an optional food group. I figured it would be hard enough to get through a day without saying no in my own home, I couldn't imagine the shenanigans that would occur on vacation.

"Wait, you're doing *what*?" Beth asked incredulously when I tried to use the "month of yes" as an excuse to get out of the trip months ago. "What the hell are you doing that for?"

"I want to see if it will change anything," I reply.

"Well now you *have* to come! I can't wait to see this in action. I am totally going to tell them to ask for ridiculous things. This is going to be awesome!"

"First of all, anything you tell them to ask for, you will be fulfilling yourself. So you just remember that. Second of all, they're going to be beasts. It's going to be all *Lord of the Flies* up in here. You'll see things you can never unsee, hear things you can never unhear. Your daughter is only four months old, what if they ask to carry her around and they drop her in the lake? I can't have this stress in my life."

"Nope, you're coming. These are the most piss-poor excuses I have ever heard. Man up and pack up – you're coming to Eagle River and that's final." Four months later, we're driving six hours north with a car full or organic groceries and fifteen gallons of natural bug repellant. Josh said "natural" bug repellent is an oxymoron as the only thing it actually repels is his sex drive, because no one wants to sleep next to a citronella-scented wife. He didn't laugh when I explained that was precisely the point – keeping pests at bay.

We pile out of the car and unpack, the kids running wild between Auntie Beth and Uncle Kevin and my parents. My mom is listening intently and responding with great animation to their tales of seeing deer on the side of the road and my dad is helping Josh unpack the car like it contains a time bomb. If there's one thing my dad doesn't allow, it's lollygagging when arriving at a vacation destination. No sir, you get that car unpacked, groceries put away, clothes in the drawers and by god, don't even think about playing with a toy unless you have put the sheets on the bed. He was also genuinely consternated by the route our GPS app took us.

"But why?" he kept musing. "It's so much more direct if you just take Highway 39 to Highway 45, turn left on County Road D, cut through the deer path off D and take the back road to where it meets 45 again. I just can't understand why it would have you take 43 to 29 to 45."

"Dad, the GPS was fine, we're here," I point out, putting approximately seventeen packages of organic hamburger buns in a pyramid on the counter. I like to be prepared for a sandwich emergency and I knew there wouldn't be organic bread in a three-hundred-mile radius of this place. "It said it was five minutes faster this way."

My father is so incensed by this statement, he pulls an old-school paper map out of his back pocket and unfurls it on the table. I can't deal with this. I leave him tracing routes with his finger, muttering to Josh about his super-secret back route. I think it involves an old fur-trading path and a sundial. Embrace the iPhone, Dad. Josh is intently looking at the map and I hear him ask my dad how far it is to Canada from here. My dad estimates about six hours and Josh's face lights up. This is so ridiculous on so many different levels.

After everyone is settled and gets some quality swimming time in, we decide to go out for dinner. Because if there's one thing a house full of food demands, it's to not be consumed. Josh quickly turns to Yelp to find us an acceptable restaurant. Josh never leaves restaurant decisions to chance. We could be in a remote mountain village in Tibet and he would declare the one restaurant in town only had seven reviews with an average of two stars, which does not meet his criteria for dining. He finds a pizza place with an acceptable level of positive reviews and we decide to head out in two different cars. Jack quickly asks if he can ride with Grandma Mary and Auntie Beth, and I say – what else – yes. Emmie hears this and pipes up for her own spot in their SUV, which I say is fine. But when Maeve asks, well, I am forced to tell her that she needs to ride with Mommy and Daddy because all the seats in Beth's car are taken. Not exactly a no, but it's certainly not a yes and probably doesn't jive with the spirit of the project.

This sets off one of the biggest tantrums I have ever seen from this child. This is what happens when a regular afternoon nap is skipped – she goes all *Exorcist* on us. She is flailing and screaming and beating her fists on the screen door trying to get outside where Jack and Emmie are climbing into the car with smug smiles on their faces. I carry her kicking and screaming out to where our car is parked and plunk her down while I open the door. My plan is to wrestle her into the car seat, strap her in and slide an iPad into her hands. As I bend down to pick her up, she rears her head upward into my chin, which causes an explosion of pain in my mouth. I drop her on the ground and scream in agony. I stagger back toward the house, blood gushing into my cupped hand. Trying to ascertain whether my tooth has gone all the way through my top lip, I make my way into the bathroom. At least I still have all my teeth, or at least I think I do. The pain is blinding.

I lean over the sink, blood dripping steadily from my mouth. I cup some water in my hand and put it up to my mouth, but I can't actually close my lips to swish it around so it just dribbles back out. My sister comes to the door in a panic and asks if I am all right. I turn and point to my lip, which has a gaping wound in it, and manage to get out, "Do I look all right?" except I can't form coherent sounds with my lips. She grabs a pink-and-green-striped baby washcloth and hands it me. "Here, bleed on this, it's fine."

In the meantime, while I am trying to stanch the bleeding, everyone else has come back into the house. Jack is genuinely empathetic for the first time in his life with tears in his eyes, Emmie is worried I am going to have to get a shot, but Maeve is not chastened in the least. She's still screaming she wants to ride in Auntie Beth's car.

"No one is riding in Auntie Beth's car because we're not going anywhere," my mom says, dropping her purse on the counter. "I'm making scrambled eggs for dinner!"

I'm losing blood like a stuck pig and my mom is whipping up a batch of scrambled eggs. Kevin whispers to my sister, "But I don't want scrambled eggs for dinner!" Beth shoots him a look and he focuses his attention on baby Lylah in her infant car seat.

At least my dad cares about me, as he comes over and assesses the damage; he thinks it could go either way on needing stitches. That will be so attractive. As my dad is peering at my lip with a mini flashlight he inexplicably has on his keychain, I hear Josh saying, "You better say sorry to Mommy. Look what you did to her. She is very sad." Maeve, however, does not feel it necessary to issue a heartfelt apology for anything. She stands ten feet away and screams, "Saw-wee!" at the top of her lungs and laughs. Josh tells her that is not a nice way to say it. She inches closer, but ratchets up the sass and the volume. I stare at her and try to remember she's three years old and didn't do it on purpose. But when she walks right up to me and spits on my foot, it becomes impossible. Josh quickly scoops her up and places her in a timeout.

I stop the bleeding by holding ice on my lip and decide I do not need actual medical attention. I walk into the living room with a bag of ice crammed on my piehole and announce we're still going out for pizza, although I clearly won't be able to eat anything for the rest of the week. There is great relief on Kevin's face as my mom puts the carton of eggs back in the refrigerator. I wordlessly get in the passenger seat of our car as Josh straps Maeve, finally quiet about the seating arrangements, in the back. When we arrive at the pizza place, Maeve starts whining that she wants to sit next to Mommy. I look at Josh with fear in my eyes and shake my head vehemently. He informs her she will be sitting at the other table with Daddy, which sets her off again. He quickly tells my mom what he wants on his pizza and removes Maeve to the car.

Jack and Emmie flank my sides at the outdoor picnic table. "Does it hurt, Mommy?" Jack asks. "Oooh, that looks like a bad owie," Emmie adds. My sister is not even attempting to conceal her laughter as I try to take a swig of beer from a bottle and it dribbles down my chin, onto my shirt. That's attractive. My mom asks the waitress for a straw, but that actually hurts more as I have to purse my lips. I settle for pouring the bottle into the right side of my mouth and looking like an idiot. Maeve comes back in just as the pizza arrives, her face red and eyes still wet. She hugs me from behind and offers a sincere, "Sorry, Mommy." She hops up on the bench across from me and waits patiently for someone to put a piece of cheese pizza on her plate.

I figure both the temperature of the food and the spiciness of the tomato sauce might send me into a pain management clinic, so I abstain from the meal. But everyone keeps raving about how great the pizza is, so I give in after about fifteen minutes and put a piece on my plate. I cut it into miniscule pieces with a knife and fork and put one tiny bite at a time in the good side of my mouth, chewing deliberately so as not to encounter the gaping wound on my lip. It takes me ten minutes to consume one slice. This must be how the "slow-food movement" was founded.

The kids are getting antsy and come over asking for ice cream. Seriously? I'm a millimeter of skin away from needing stitches and I'm still subjected to the constraints of my pledge? I say yes and we all troop down to the old-time ice cream parlor on the main drag. "Can I have bubble gum ice cream?" Emmie asks. Awesome. My child who has never been allowed to chew gum, is now going to chew gum while eating ice cream. "Go for it," I respond and she jumps around clapping her hands. I order myself a dish of salted caramel ice cream and quickly realize how difficult it is to eat from a spoon when you can't purse your lips. I get creative and end up using the spoon upside down, licking the ice cream off the underside rather than using my lips to pull it off the bowl of the spoon. It takes me three times as long as everyone else to finish and by the end, I throw some of it away because it's all melted and gross.

The fun that night doesn't stop with my bloody lip. It doesn't even begin to stop there. The fun continues when Josh and Kevin return from the grocery store after the kids are in bed with only one type of beer – a beer that nobody even asked for.

"Really? Labatt Blue? That's all they had?" I ask as Josh smiles wickedly.

"Strangest thing, isn't it, honey? They must have the fever up here, just like me," he replies, cracking open a can. Not only did he buy gross beer, he bought gross beer *in cans*. It's like we've never met before.

"The fever? What exactly is 'the fever?'"

"The Canadian fever. That must be why they only stock Canadian beer at the grocery store."

Please note, we're in Wisconsin. I'm shocked they stock anything other than Miller products and local craft beers.

"Where's my Spotted Cow?" I ask shrilly. "I specifically asked for Spotted Cow. There is no way they only had Labatt's – you probably drove to four places to even find it." New Glarus Brewing's Spotted Cow is my most favorite beer, sold only in Wisconsin, and I can't get enough of it when we're north of the Illinois state line. What the hell is he trying to prove with this Labatt's crap?

"Listen, we're so close to the motherland up here that people get the Canadian fever and they start craving all things Canadian, even beer," Josh says, taking a long slug of his beer.

"We aren't even that close to Canada," I retort. "Have you ever looked at a map? Or heard of a little body of water called Lake Superior? Have you? Because you'd have to cross it to get to Canada from here."

"Do you know how many people have died trying to escape this country by swimming across that lake to make it to the Promised Land?" Josh traces the red maple leaf on his can with his fingernail.

"I do know. Zero."

"Don't talk about my dead brothers like they're nothing. They fought the good fight. If that lake had just been frozen, they could have skated across and would still be alive today."

"Zilch. None. Never happened," I continue, ignoring him.

"How can you be so sure? The American government has covered it all up. They don't want everyone knowing about the Canadian defection problem. I'm pretty sure more people die trying to swim across Lake Superior than from Florida to Cuba."

"You have that backwards – Cubans swim to the U.S., not the other way around. I'm quite sure no Americans are risking their lives to make it to Cuban soil."

"Jay Z and Beyonce did," Josh interrupts.

"Jay Z and Beyonce vacationed there after flying in on their private jet. I'm positive they didn't swim there from Florida under the cover of darkness, Josh. And besides, any idiot trying to sneak into Canada is going to be smart enough to go through Minnesota or Michigan *by land* rather than cross the largest lake in the world."

"You think? So I might be the first?"

"Oh, you'd be the first. Of that, I have no doubt."

Josh toasts Kevin, who can't keep a straight face when Josh declares he's pouring some out for his dead Canadian homies. I can't keep a straight face, either, but I'm not smiling, I'm fuming with indignation. And craving a cold beer. I stomp upstairs, leaving Josh and Kevin in the lower level of the house to enjoy their frosty Labatt's in front of the Brewers game. Because nothing says quality time in the northwoods of Wisconsin like lying around inside watching cable TV. If it wasn't for the stupid liquor laws in Wisconsin, I would have gone out to get my own Spotted Cow, but one can't buy alcohol after nine o'clock, so I had to settle for sulking with a brandy old fashioned that my Mommy made me. Sometimes, moms know exactly what you need.

Unfortunately, the alcohol does nothing to dull the pain of my gaping lip wound. I wake up several times during the night, my top lip throbbing, literally stuck to my bottom lip. Pulling the sensitive skin apart is torture. I wake up when a little face appears at my bedside at six in the morning. "Mommy, what hoppen to you lip?" Maeve asks seriously. Oh my god. Are you kidding me?

Sitting on the pier watching the kids that afternoon I began to shift blame from Maeve and assign it to myself. This might be a symptom of Stockholm Syndrome, but it makes sense. If I had simply followed my own rules, none of this would have happened and I would happily be applying lip gloss right now. Instead, I said no and all hell broke loose. I could have easily asked Beth and Kevin to move a car seat to the third row. Sure, it would have been a pain and it would have required more time, but in the end, we spent an extra thirty minutes running triage on my lip. It would have been quicker to just let her ride with everyone else.

It took an entire week before the wound healed over and I still have a bump on the inside of my lip months later. Every time I run my tongue over the bump, it's a tangible reminder of my failure to follow my own rules. And every once in a while Maeve will say to me, "Mommy, remember when I hurted your lip? I sorry." So I guess we all learned a lesson in the end.

CHAPTER THIRTEEN
SHE'LL HAVE THE ROCKS, WELL-DONE, WITH A SIDE OF SAND

Kids have disgusting habits. They gleefully pick their noses, unabashedly grab their crotches at inopportune moments, lick food from their filthy hands and have no problem touching every square inch of a public restroom toilet. Sometimes, if you're really lucky, they do all of those things at the same time.

It's no wonder they're constantly sick, what with all the hands in the mouths and licking of seats on public transportation. And yes, my son once actually sucked on the top of a plastic molded seat on the Chicago L train before I noticed what he was doing. My Mother of the Year trophy is proudly displayed in the living room. Where do you keep yours?

When Maeve was finally able to run about on her own, we discovered she liked to put stuff in her mouth. Bouncy balls, Bey Blades, Disney figurines, watches, pinecones, quarters and one time, three Hungry Hungry Hippos marbles. That one nearly sent me to the emergency room for an electrocardiogram. I couldn't imagine why Maeve suddenly had very white, very large, very round teeth in her little mouth. The big kids never played Hungry Hungry Hippos again.

But Maeve's favorite thing to put in her mouth was – and still is – sand. When she was a wee toddler, I put her down in the sandbox one day and showed her how to shovel sand from the ground into a bucket. She clapped and demanded I hand her a shovel of her own and she mimicked my efforts. I figured we had a champion sandcastle builder on our hands and readied myself for the engineering scholarships that would surely come her way. Then instead of putting the sand in the bucket, she brought the shovel to her mouth.

"No! Yucky! We do not eat sand!" I admonished, removing her from the sandbox and redirecting her to the slide. And of course, being sixteen months old at the time, she took my reaction and ran with it. Then, every time we went to the park, she hightailed it to the sandbox and started eating sand as quickly as her little arms would deliver it. We tried everything: redirection, timeouts, modeling, but nothing worked. My friend Leah is the one who scared me straight.

"You know, Natalie's kids got pinworms in that sandbox," she confided one day as she watched me scoop a sand-covered and screaming Maeve out of the sandbox by her armpits. But when Leah says "pinworms" in her Georgia drawl, it makes them sound fun, like something one might find at a garden party or a cotillion in the South. "I won't let my girls anywhere near it."

"Oh my god!" I screeched. "That's disgusting!"

"Wait 'til you see actual pinworms, then you'll be disgusted all right," she shuddered.

After the pinworm discussion, Maeve was banned from that park altogether. For an entire year, we took her to a different playground down the street. The big kids cried and pleaded, "We want to go to the big park!" but I stood firm. I even joked to our pediatrician at Maeve's yearly checkup that I thought she had pica and he didn't laugh.

"What do you mean?" he asked seriously.

"Oh, well, she eats sand every time we go to the park," I explained. "And dirt. And rocks. She's clearly only doing it for the attention."

"Or for the iron content," he replied. He stuck her tiny heel with a needle for a blood draw a few minutes later and my poor baby's test results came back showing she was severely anemic. Then the child who eagerly ate dirt refused to let a liquid iron supplement touch her lips. After a few weeks of sneaking it into chocolate pudding and smoothies and convincing her to eat raw spinach salads like her brother and sister, her iron count was back to normal and she actually stopped eating dirt.

But the sand eating continued unabated. I figured out by this point, the sand was all about attention. We still avoided the big park when possible, unless we were going to the waterpark, so when Jack and Emmie ask to go to the big park this morning, I grit my teeth and smile. "Sure," I say, "let's do it!" The excitement level is kicked up to ten and they're running around like crazy people. Jack and Emmie are beside themselves because they know this is too good to be true; Maeve is plotting her appetizer of rocks followed by a main course of sand and a dessert of mud pie.

After a fun-filled two-block walk including pushing, shoving, accusations of cheating and crying over a lost race, we arrive at the park red-faced (the kids) and annoyed (me). Jack and Emmie take off for the swings with cries of, "Mommy! Push me!" trailing over their shoulders. I grab Maeve by the hand and offer to push her, too. But she shouts, "No! I'm playing on the slide!" Knock yourself out, sweetie. Not literally, of course, but you know what I mean.

I take turns being bossed around by the big kids, each begging for more pushes and underdogs. I am their Swing Bitch, unable to say no. I keep one eye on Maeve on the climbing equipment and notice a few minutes later she's not there. My eyes scan the length of the playground and find her in the shade of the sandbox, happily digging away. I sprint over, leaving the protests of "no fair" in my wake to find Maeve two-fisting some shovels, her face covered in sand.

Like the standoff in the O.K. Corral, I stand still and stare at her, saying nothing. She coolly looks me in the eye and puts a shovelful of sand in her mouth, then laughs, the sand sticking to her tongue and face, running down the front of her shirt. Another mom looks up and stifles her laugh. I have nothing in my repertoire to stop this; I'm simply along for the ride. "Taste good?" I ask Maeve, holding my ground with my arms crossed across my chest.

"Mrrmmmhrumm," she says through a mouthful of sand. I silently wonder how contagious pinworms are and whether or not she can give them to me. I inspect my cuticles, trying my best to ignore her antics. Another mom, who has no idea Maeve's mommy is standing right here, gently says, "Oh sweetie, that's yucky." Maeve stares her down with a look of loathing and the mom turns back to her own son. This child will cut you.

Jack runs over to ask me to watch him on the monkey bars and does a double-take. "Mommy! Maeve is eating sand!" You don't say? He panics and climbs into the sandbox, grabbing the shovel from Maeve. "Maeve! No! Don't eat the sand or Mommy will make us go home! Mommy! I don't want to go home. Please don't make us!" Maeve is screeching and tugging on the shovel, while Jack is pleading with her to stop eating sand. Emmie wanders over to find out what all the commotion is about and runs the other way when she sees Maeve leaning down to the ground and shoving handfuls of sand in her mouth as fast as she can. Her eyes are wild and Jack is practically pulling her arm out of her socket trying to stop her.

"Jack, leave her alone," I say. "We're not leaving."

"But Maeve is eating sand," he cries. "We have to."

"Don't worry about it," I say. "Maeve, you let me know when you're done. I'm going to be right over here with Jack and Emmie." With that, I turn and walk away, leaving Miss Sandman to her own devices. And you know what? It's actually pretty freeing. I've spent two years of my life begging her to stop eating sand, giving her negative attention for doing so, reinforcing the bad behavior. If she wants to eat sand, then that's her problem. Well, her problem and the pinworms. And potentially the neighborhood cats who use the sand as a litterbox. Maybe this isn't such a good idea after all.

I sneak a look over at her from where I'm standing at the monkey bars and see she's abandoned her all-you-can-eat buffet. She's sitting dumbfounded, wondering where the hell all the attention just went. She stands up, brushes herself off and heads over to where I'm standing. I feign surprise when she hugs my leg and ask if she's having fun.

"Mommy! I eat the sand!" she says, looking at me for a reaction.

"You did?" I ask nonchalantly.

She doesn't know how to react. "Mommy, I eat the sand, I said." She wants to be absolutely sure I know the status of what's happened here.

"Yes, I know." I don't even glance in her direction. "Wow, Jack, great job!"

Maeve plops down at my feet and screws her face up. "Mommy. I. Ate. Sand." She enunciates every word. She must figure I've missed something here.

"Maeve. I. Know." I enunciate right back at her.

Maeve reluctantly goes over to the swings and belly-flops down on one, forlornly swinging herself back and forth. She eventually mopes over to where Jack and Emmie are playing a complicated game of dinosaur tag and sits on the bottom of the slide. This is genius! I should have done this months ago.

After her self-imposed exile from play, she can no longer watch as the other kids run and scream and she gets up and starts chasing the big kids, forgetting all about it. I'm finally able to take a seat on a nearby faux rock formation and assess my victory. This Yes Mommy thing is working out beautifully. The kids are happy and healthy (future pinworms aside) and, for the most part, behaving normally. I'm not sure this is really sinking in as an automatic parenting strategy, however, as my stress level is still through the roof when I'm confronted with a truly awful situation where I can't say *no*, *don't* or *stop*. I can kind of see why people actually choose to parent like this day in and day out. I mean sure, when Jack was a baby, we vowed not to say "no" because we didn't want to stifle his creativity or his exploration of his world. I think I read some ridiculous parenting book that dispensed this advice, but the first time he tried to touch the fireplace, that theory went right out the window.

But is it easier because I'm not fighting a million little battles every day and ignoring conventional rules? It's pretty easy to let the kids watch TV all day and eat crap whenever they want. Hell, that would be my dream day, too. But is this what's best for them in the long run? How do they become functioning members of society without learning to follow rules? They sure won't have Yes Teacher this fall or Yes Coach when they're at soccer practice and hopefully they never have to find out if our local law enforcement branch employs a Yes Officer. But, I remind myself, they are experiencing natural consequences for their actions.

I'm feeling pretty positive about the whole situation as I round the kids up so we can head home. I can do this! I should have done a Year of Yes! My kids are going to learn how to make good decisions and I won't be that helicopter parent I read about in *The New York Times* who stays up until three in the morning building science fair projects and writes her kids' college term papers. This shit is easy. As the kids sit and shake the sand out of their sandals before we leave, Maeve takes one last furtive handful of sand and throws it in her mouth. I don't say a word.

And then something so evil and so awful happens it stops me cold in my tracks. I hear the soft tinkles of the ice cream truck. In my estimation, he's about three-quarters of a block away and I wonder if we have time to escape. I beg the children to hurry up, but possessing ears that haven't been damaged by years of concerts and kids screaming directly into them, they also hear the strains of "The Entertainer" by Scott Joplin. Every single time my kids hear or see the ice cream truck, they ask if they can get something. Let me be clear, we have never, not a single time, actually gotten anything from the ice cream truck. But every time they see it, they ask and the answer is always the same: no, no you may not have a fifteen-dollar package of high-fructose corn syrup and red dye on a stick. We will go home and have organic fruit popsicles or ice cream, but we are not getting anything here. The ice cream truck even parks next to our school each afternoon during the spring and fall months – you haven't lived until you've watched your child watch his best friend slowly enjoy every last lick of a neon-yellow Sponge Bob ice cream pop while your child stands empty-handed next to him. I even asked the principal to get the truck booted from the area, and while she agreed it was awful, she doesn't have jurisdiction on city streets. Total bummer.

I know what's coming before I even hear it. "Mommy! Mommy! Mommy! Can we get ice cream?" They say it in unison and so quickly I can't believe their mouths can align with their brains that quickly. They certainly never answer with such speed when I ask who crushed a granola bar in the couch cushions.

I take a deep breath. The kids are wildly jumping around, expectantly looking at my face. I take another deep breath. Man, this really sucks. But does it? Seriously, it's *ice cream*. It will bring immense joy to my children. I need to get ahold of myself.

"Yes!" I say, and the children spontaneously combust in front of me. It's like they're watching The Beatles on *The Ed Sullivan Show* in 1964. I urge them to please calm down and choose something from the menu. Maeve immediately chooses the Dora pop, Jack practically rips the Sponge Bob bar out of the man's hand and Emmie's eyes light up when I assure her that yes, she can indeed have a Choco Taco. I fork over my eight dollars and fifty cents and treat my kids to their very own "when I was a kid" moment.

"When I was little, the ice cream truck used to come to our street only once a summer and the treats were fifty cents," I explain. They ignore me, focused on their creamy, cold treats. I vividly remember running down the block as fast as my legs would carry me, chasing after a truck that had no interest in stopping. My kids see the damn truck on a daily basis – where's the specialness in that?

Jack is actually biting off pieces of Sponge Bob and I cringe, wondering at what age tooth sensitivity sets in. Emmie is happily nibbling at the edges of her chocolatey goodness when catastrophe strikes Maeve. As she takes a bite of Dora's hair, the entire pop falls off the stick and lands with a thud on the ground, immediately starting to melt into a sad brown puddle. The pause before the scream starts is so long, I actually consider the idea she might pass out and then it comes, blood-curdling and about fifty decibels greater than a jet engine. I immediately bend down and hug her, assuring her it's okay. Sobs wrack her little body and she clings to my neck crying, "My Dora pop! My Dora pop!" She's really batting a thousand today.

Emmie coolly looks over at the situation and announces through a mouthful of Choco Taco, "I'm not sharing mine." I can always count on Emmie to be generous with her siblings. Except when it involves toys, food or money. But ask her to share her salad and she's all over it. Jack is covered in some sort of yellow goo. His face, his hands, his white shirt and even his sandals have taken a direct hit. Thankfully we don't have a younger sibling who needs his hand-me-downs because he's one-and-done with his clothes. He finishes the last bite of his pop and says, "Sorry, Maeve, mine is all gone." This, of course, produces a fresh round of screaming, now with, "Jack won't share with me" thrown in for good measure.

I know the only way to make this stop, so I pony up another two dollars and fifty cents for a fresh Dora pop. Maeve stops screaming when I present her with the new treat and eagerly sits down next to me on a bench after I suggest this will prevent another tragedy. She tentatively bites Dora bit by bit, which is great for keeping her off the sidewalk, but not so great for keeping her from dripping all over Maeve's hands. I look at Emmie, who is licking her fingers, and see she has a goatee of chocolate. I've got one stained yellow, two stained brown, I'm out eleven bucks, my kids are now full of high-fructose corn syrup and food dye and it's not even dinner time. What an outstanding afternoon. This is what I get for feeling positive.

Just then, my friend, Heather, arrives with her four kids in tow. She surveys the situation and gasps. Heather feels the same way I do about the ice cream truck.

"You didn't!" she says, gesturing to the truck.

"Oh, I did," I say dejectedly.

"Why on earth?" she asks, her eyes wide.

"Yes Mommy," I say simply. My friends all know about the project and ask for daily updates. Then they laugh at my stupidity. They all know better than to stop saying no.

"Damn."

"Yeah. We gotta go. Maeve ate a truckload of sand and then the ice cream man came. I need to get them in the house before anything else happens."

Heather salutes me as I round the three kids up. "Godspeed," she laughs.

CHAPTER FOURTEEN
CURLING CAMP ISN'T FOR BEAUTICIANS

"What's that man doing?" Jack asks from the backseat as we exit the highway one afternoon.

I look over to see a man holding a sign. He's wearing tattered jeans and a torn, dirty T-shirt and no shoes. His beard is gray and mangy and his baseball cap is so filthy the logo is no longer recognizable. He's covered in a layer of grime, holding a sign that says, "Homeless vet. Please help."

To be completely honest, we see men and women in this position all the time at freeway exit ramps in the city. Sometimes they're homeless veterans, sometimes couples, usually single men, and one heart-wrenching time, a mother and a young child. They wander between the cars, sometimes holding an empty cup, trying to make eye contact with drivers and passengers who normally look anywhere but directly at them. I've driven by these people so many times they have become a part of the scenery of our drive, their carts and bedrolls parked under the overpasses blending in to the concrete walls. I'm embarrassed to say that I don't make eye contact with them, that I don't roll down the window and drop change in their cups. But I have chosen to give back in other ways – by organizing and giving to food drives, by volunteering at community shelters, by donating to organizations that help the homeless with services such as health care and housing. But I don't give money to people on the street.

When the kids were younger, it was easy to avoid the topic. But now that they're older and more aware of what is going on in the world around them, it's more difficult. And to answer Jack's question about what that man was doing was going to take a multi-faceted approach.

"Well, I think he's homeless and he's asking people for money," I say, employing advice I've seen about not giving kids more information than they ask for. Just the facts, ma'am.

"Why does he need money?" Emmie asks. "Doesn't he have a daddy who works?"

Oh, Emily, you really know how to make a stay-at-home mom feel special.

"Well grown-ups don't get money from their mommies and daddies," I say. "They have to earn money to pay for their own things. Sometimes if people don't have jobs, they can't pay for their houses or for food, so they ask other people to help them out."

"But you don't have a job, how do you get money?" Emmie helpfully asks. Seriously with this child.

Jack butts in. "She gets money from Daddy because he has a job."

"Excuse me, but I *do* have a job and it's taking care of all of you. Who do you think cooks dinner and cleans up after you and makes sure we have food to eat and clean clothes to wear?"

"And you're a writer, too!" Jack adds. "You make money from that."

Daddy would disagree on exactly what constitutes "making money" but yes, I tell him, being a writer is my job, too. Emmie gives me the side-eye in the rearview mirror and I realize this child really needs some schooling in the home economics arts. Listen, kid, somebody needs to peruse Pinterest for hours on end to find those amazing little clothespin/coffee filter/butterfly crafts you make in school. They don't just create themselves.

"But we're very lucky that we have money so we can pay for our house and our food and have clean clothes and do fun things," I say, seizing a teachable moment when I see one. "Not everybody gets to go to Disneyworld or Hawaii on vacation. Not everybody gets to go skiing in the winter or to waterparks in the summer. Not everybody gets to eat at Chipotle whenever he wants. You are very, very fortunate to have the ability to do those things."

"But why didn't you give the man any money?" Jack asks, circling back because I clearly didn't give him the real answer he was looking for.

I hesitate, but decide honesty is the best policy. "Because we help people in different ways and I don't think giving people money actually helps them. I think giving people food and a place to sleep is probably better for them." At this point, we're already in the driveway and getting out of the car.

"I have some money from my allowance," Jack says. "I could give it to him."

I stop walking and look at his earnest face. He's totally serious.

"Jack, that is the nicest thing I have ever heard you say," I say, hugging him.

He smiles. "Can we go back right now?"

Yes, yes we absolutely can. For once, I don't hesitate before I say it.

After running full-speed through the house and almost falling down the stairs on the way back down from his room, we're back in the car, driving toward the highway. Emmie got into the action as well, offering to donate a quarter and Maeve is clutching a penny in her hot little hand. We approach the intersection at the highway and see the same man on the opposite side of the median at the bottom of the off-ramp. The light turns red for our line of traffic and the man moves to our side of the intersection. I roll down the back window and Jack leans out to drop fifty cents in the cup – a quarter from him and one from Emmie. The man wordlessly nods, but Maeve starts screaming because she wants to put her penny in the cup herself, and refuses to let Jack do it for her.

The light turns green and all hell breaks out in the car. The people behind me are honking, but Maeve is screaming like someone is branding her with a cattle prod. This is exactly why I don't do nice things – they always backfire. I swivel in my seat as deeply as I can, holding out my hand and begging Maeve, "Just give me the penny, please, honey, give me the penny." She holds it out of my reach in her fat little fist as traffic continues to pile up behind me. People are honking like we're in a parade, but no one is throwing candy or waving like Miss America. The homeless man starts to wander away and I yell, "No! Wait!" as I stab the button to turn the flashers on and use the driver's control to open the window next to Maeve. "Would you mind going around so my daughter can give you something?"

The man shuffles around to the curb side and Maeve flings the penny at him, missing the cup. My three-year-old daughter has just thrown a practically worthless piece of copper at a homeless person. He looks down and picks up the penny and nods at Maeve, who is beaming like she's delivered presents on Christmas morning. I roll up the windows and drive through the intersection, hanging my head in shame.

"Mommy, we did it!" Jack said excitedly.

"We did, Jackie," I acknowledge, thankful he doesn't realize how embarrassing it is that I asked a homeless man to walk around my car so my child could give him a penny. It's the thought that counts though, right? Trying to rationalize it only makes me feel worse, so I choose to focus on the positive. My kids did the right thing; they saw someone in need and tried to help. Isn't that what one strives for as a parent, that the children learn empathy and practice kindness? That they share their time or talents or riches?

They're so excited to tell Josh about their adventure when they see him. Emmie runs into the house, bounds up to Josh and throws her arms over her head. "We gave lots of money to a man!" she yells. Josh cocks his eyebrow at me.

"They gave fifty cents to the homeless guy by the highway," I explain. "They're high on giving right now."

"You know what I'm high on? Life," Josh says.

"Oh really? Do tell," I say with curiosity.

"I'm just a lucky guy. I have a beautiful wife and three great children."

"What do you want?" I ask suspiciously. He's never this nice without an agenda.

"Me? What do I want? I have everything I could ever need, what could I possibly want that I don't already have?"

Now I know he's fishing for something. He crosses the room and kisses me, making the kids giggle. "Why are you kissing Mommy?" Maeve asks.

"Because I love her," Josh responds, kissing me again.

"Did you fall and hit your head?" I ask, feeling his noggin for bumps. "Have you taken drugs of some sort? Oh my god, did someone slip you Ecstasy? They totally did. Don't you know how dangerous that is? You have children, for god's sake!"

"Because I kiss and hug my wife, I am under suspicion of drug use? Real nice, Amy. But no, I am completely sober."

"I'm not doing another day of Yes Wife, if that's what you're angling for," I tell him.

"This has nothing to do with your little project," he responds. "I have some very exciting news. Kids, gather 'round, Daddy has an announcement." The kids barely look up from their iPod Touches. "Daddy found curling camps for you on the Internet!" Josh's face is practically glowing with excitement.

I stare at him, counting to ten in my head.

"Guys, didn't you hear me, you can go to curling camp next summer!"

Emmie pauses her Minion Rush game and asks him, deadpan, "We're going to a camp for people with curly hair?"

Josh runs his hands over the length of his face. "No. Curling is a sport that's popular in lots of countries, including Canada. You spin little rocks toward a goal on the ice."

"So do you get to wear a fancy ice-skating dress?" Emmie asks excitedly. Emmie plays tennis strictly for the apparel and has been begging us for ice skating lessons so she can wear the dresses like she sees on TV. Our very own budding Dorothy Hamill, except for the fact Emmie despised her learn-to-skate hockey lessons and refused to let go of the little walker for two straight eight-week sessions.

"No, no dresses," Josh says.

"Then forget it," Emmie mutters.

"Is it like hockey?" Jack asks.

"No, there's no skating," Josh answers.

"So how do you not fall on the ice?" Jack asks.

"I don't know. I guess you just glide carefully. That's not the point. The point is you can learn all about it next summer at curling camp!"

Maeve cheers lustily and claps. She's such a Daddy's girl. Josh grabs her for a hug.

"I don't wanna go to curling camp," Jack says. "I want to do LEGO camp next summer." Of course, because he needs me to shell out three-hundred bucks for him to play with LEGOs for a week, which he can do for free in the comfort of our own home. But then I would have to supervise him all day, so yeah, LEGO camp sounds awesome.

"Yeah and I'm not going to camp next summer at all," Emmie says. "I'm staying home with Mommy all day!"

"You know what? Curling camp sounds super. Maybe Mommy will go to curling camp next summer and Daddy can stay home with all of you!" I announce. Trust me, nobody is staying home with Mommy all day next summer. If it means curling camp is on the docket, then everybody grab a broom and get ready for the bonspiel!

"Look, let me show you what curling is," Josh says, giving me a dirty look. He tries to grab the iPad from Maeve and sends her into a tizzy of tears. "Maeve, I just want to show you something on the Internet. Calm down. Give me the iPad. Maeve, give it to me. No, do not kick me. That's not nice. I'm just trying to show you something cool!"

Josh is visibly annoyed and stamps off to the kitchen, iPadless and defeated.

"This is all your fault," he says as I follow him.

"My fault?" I say laughing. "I didn't do anything. Like our kids are actually going to curling camp. Come on!"

"It's like soccer camp in Canada, everybody does it."

"That is ridiculous! And so untrue."

"It is not."

I pull my phone from my back pocket and wave it in Josh's face. I quickly ask one of my Facebook friends, who happens to reside in Canada. "Ah, no. Not even close. But, Ringette camp is something I could get behind."

"What's Ringette camp?" Josh asks, his curiosity getting the best of him.

"What? I thought you knew everything about Canada. And you don't even know what Ringette camp is? They're going to revoke your Visa."

"You don't need a Visa to visit Canada. How did you even graduate high school?"

"I will remind you I went to *private* school because my parents loved me more than yours loved you, public-school boy."

"This is why I can't have conversations with you. Our own children go to public school and you can't stop raving about their education. Do you even think before words come flying out of your mouth?"

"Whatever. I do know, however, that nobody goes to curling camp but lots of girls go to Ringette camp, so you can—" I stop short of saying "suck it" because they kids are in the room and smile sweetly.

"Mommy, is Ringette camp where you wear jewelry all day?" Emmie asks. "Because I would really like that camp!"

"No, sorry Em, it's hockey camp just for girls. Would you like to go?"

Emmie blanches. "No! I told you I don't like hockey! I want to go to ice skating camp so I can wear a pretty dress." And we've come full circle.

"Listen, no one is going anywhere to camp," I say. "You're all going down the block to the park for day camp like you have every summer and that's the end of it."

"*They're going* to *curling camp*," Josh hisses.

We'll see about that.

CHAPTER FIFTEEN
THERE'S A SKEEBALL SCHOLARSHIP
IN HIS FUTURE

It's a beautiful day in Chicago. The sun is shining, there's not a cloud in the sky and a breeze off the lake is holding temperatures in the upper seventies. It's a day made for eating lunch outside, for slathering on sunscreen, for ditching the car for a walk, for sending your children to summer camp so you can sprawl out on the lawn furniture and read a book in peace. I'm making the lunches for camp when Jack runs in to the kitchen and opens the junk drawer looking for a stapler.

"Why do you need a stapler?" I ask him, spreading sunflower-seed butter on whole wheat bread. God forbid a child these days should come within a three-mile radius of a peanut.

"My pajamas ripped," he says.

"You don't staple pajamas," I explain. "You sew them. Well, someone sews them. Not me. I don't know how to sew. You should ask Grandpa Scott, he knows how."

Instead of a stapler, which I'm pretty sure we don't have anyway, Jack pulls out a plastic Ziploc bag of Chuck E. Cheese's tokens and tickets. I know it sounds hard to believe, but we once left that den of germs and tantrums with a surplus. I believe there was a threat to leave if someone couldn't stop acting crazy, which was actually carried out, so the tokens and tickets came home with us and were stuffed out of sight.

"Are these Chuck E. Cheese's tokens?" Jack asks excitedly.

"I have no idea," I lie.

"Well they have a picture of Chuck E. Cheese on them," he says.

"Well then, that settles it," I say. "I guess they are." I slice the sandwiches in halves and grab a handful of carrots for each child, dropping them into their Planet Box containers along with some blueberries.

"Mommy can we please go to Chuck E. Cheese's today?" Jack says. "Please?"

I would rather douse myself in gasoline and strike a match. I hesitate before asking, "But what about camp? You all have camp today!"

"No, I want to go to Chuck E. Cheese's instead of camp," Jack pleads.

Emmie hears the discussion and chimes in that she would also like to skip camp and hit the arcade. Maeve is too busy playing with the iPad to care what the heck we're discussing, but the big kids put on the full-court press.

"Sure, let's do it," I say, thanking my lucky stars we only send one of them to a tuition-based camp; Maeve goes to camp at her amazing preschool and while it's not breaking the bank, it's also just pricey enough per day that I don't appreciate her missing.

I know that the Cheese is best visited when the doors are first unlocked at the fine hour of half past nine. There's nobody there but the staff members, and they're all still wiping the surfaces down with disinfectant. We once attended a birthday party at five o'clock on a Saturday night and it was pandemonium. There was a line out the door to get in, and this was the middle of winter! Kids were screaming and crying, adults were jockeying for position at the ticket counter and some snotty-nosed child tried to steal Jack's stream of tickets from the Skeeball machine. I vowed we'd never go back, but my friend, Maureen, turned me on to the beauty of going first thing in the morning. She brings snacks for her kids, sets them loose with twenty dollars in tokens and they have the place to themselves.

I reluctantly tell everyone to get his or her shoes on and put the lunches in the fridge. Maeve refuses to move from her perch on the ottoman and ignores my second request for shoes. Hey, no skin off my back if she doesn't want to go. I wander over to my computer and start reading "Get Off My Internets," which is like the *National Enquirer* for mommy bloggers. If there's scandal or snark about something someone has posted on a blog, this site has the details and the commenters have a field day with the rest. I'm not an everyday reader, but sometimes, a girl just needs to pass the time with some good old-fashioned blog gossip. I'm able to scan several posts before Jack and Emmie ratchet the whining up to levels I can no longer easily ignore.

"Moooooommmmmmmmmmmmyyyyyyyyy," Emmie says, dragging each syllable out to infinity, "I want to gooooooooooooo."

"Well, I would love to take you, but your sister is still sitting in the living room with the iPad and no shoes," I say, shrugging my shoulders.

"Maeve," Jack screams, "get your shoes on!"

"No," she says. That's it, no discussion, just one word. This one will make an awesome mediator some day.

Emmie gets Maeve's sandals from the shoe rack near the back door and runs into the living room with them. Maeve doesn't even find it necessary to answer Emmie's inquiries into why she's still sitting there playing *Where's My Water* like it's her job, she totally ignores her. This so incenses Emmie that she chucks the sandals at Maeve's head. Seeing as I have limited power of authority in this situation without use of the word "stop," I stay out of it, but listen from afar. And that's not hard to do considering the level of screaming that is coming from the living room. I peek in to see Emmie sitting on top of Maeve's legs, trying to shove her foot in a sandal. Maeve is writhing and hitting Emmie on the back, screaming, "No! Stop it! You're hurting me!" Jack is blissfully ignoring the chaos having commandeered the iPad.

"Girls, someone is going to get hurt," I say. "Emmie, please let Maeve put her own shoes on. Maeve, please use your words instead of your fists." I lift Emmie off Maeve and separate them. I sit down in front of Maeve and pretend to put her sandals on my own feet, prompting her to laugh.

"What?" I ask innocently. "I'm ready to go. Come on. Wait, why don't these sandals fit over my toes? Did my sandals shrink?"

Maeve grabs the sandal from my hands and yells, "Mommy, deese are mine!"

"No, those can't be yours. Those are mine."

"No, Mommy, they don't fit you."

"Well if they fit you, then you better hurry up and put them on."

She's shoed like a horse in mere seconds and we're ready to hit the road. I shove the baggie of tokens in my purse and grab my keys. Of course we can't enter the car without more drama. Maeve, who sits in the outside backseat on the driver's side shoves her way into the car first, creating a logjam for everyone else who comes after her. Our parking setup only allows us to enter on one side of the car, so Maeve blocking the way results in Jack shoving past her to get to his seat and Emmie is howling because Maeve has stuck her legs out in front of her, blocking Emmie from getting in. As Emmie tries to push her way past, Maeve gives her a shove, and Emmie falls off the running board onto the ground. Maeve smirks at her and says, "Ha ha, Emmie." I swear to god, if this was a normal month, they'd be back in the house faster than they could say Whack-A-Mole. Emmie kicks Maeve in the face when she climbs into her own seat in the third row and now both of them are howling. Good times.

Emmie sniffles her way into her seat with a shove to Maeve's shoulder for good measure and I buckle the instigator in to her seat despite her protestations of "I can do it myself!" Yes, I know. But I'm not in the mood to wait another eight minutes right now. We finally pull away from the house and arrive at the germnasium without further incident. I turn to the back and go over the rules.

"Just to be clear, I'm going to give everybody a cup of tokens and once they're gone, they're gone," I say. "Everybody stays together. Everybody takes turns. Everybody thanks Mommy for this amazing day."

They all sing-song "thank you Mommy" in unison and everyone holds hands as we cross the parking lot. I wistfully look up at the cloudless sky and ask one more time, "Are you guys sure you don't want to go to the park instead?" They shout "no" as we come to the entrance – shocker. Before I open the glass door, I whip out a bottle of hand sanitizer and hose everyone down. We're as ready as we'll ever be.

A bored high-school-aged employee informs us we all need matching numbered stamps on the inside of our wrists and I raise my eyebrows in question. "It's so no one takes a kid that doesn't belong to him," she says, snapping her gum.

"But you can't see them," I point out before she grabs a blacklight and shows me my stupidity. Alrighty then. She unlatches the red velvet rope and the kids immediately swarm around me begging for tokens. We head over to the counter where I fork over my credit card so we can play more than seven games and I dole out cups of tokens to each kid. The minute the cups leave my hands, they're off, forgetting the first rule, which was everyone stays together. Damn it. Thankfully, we're one of only three families in the joint, so I can easily keep my eye on them. Maeve runs back to me and drags me by the hand to a miniature carousel, asking me to help her climb up. You'd think she's riding a real horse, err, mouse, with her level of enthusiasm. I see Jack is spinning some *Wheel of Fortune*-type game and I finally see Emmie's feet in the giant tunnel maze above our heads. This isn't so bad.

"Mommy, I hafta go potty," Maeve says, grabbing her shorts. Of course she does.

"Why didn't you go at home?" I ask exasperatedly. Although I know the answer: because she has a plan to visit every public restroom in the United States, and that includes Hawaii, where she knocked quite a few off her list during a family vacation last summer. "Oh, come on. Hurry up."

I drag her by the hand over to the *Deal or No Deal* game that Jack is now playing and ask him to please come with me to the bathroom. "But I don't have to go," he says, never taking his eyes off the computer-generated suitcases full of tickets.

"Listen, I can't leave you alone and I'm certainly not sending your sister into a public bathroom alone," I snap. "Finish the game and let's go." By this time, Maeve is grabbing her crotch and doing the potty dance. I don't even ask Emmie to join us, I just grab her by the hand as I walk by the basketball game and drag her along with us. Maeve screams, "I can do it myself!" so I stand outside the stall and wait. And I wait and I wait and I wait some more. Jack shows me he's learned nothing about recycling and reducing waste at school by pulling a length of brown paper towel out of the machine that is longer than he is. I frown at him, but say nothing, so he moves on to the sink, where he runs the water for no apparent reason. Again, this child has no problem wasting our precious resources. Shameful.

"Maeve, what are you doing in there?" I ask, sticking my eye in front of the crack between the door and wall. The answer, I can plainly see, is she's running her hands around the circumference of the toilet seat.

"Maeve! Sto— N— I mean, uh, come out of there right now!" I rattle the door and watch as she laughs.

"Mommy, my hands are like racecars and this is the track," she says gleefully. Oh dear lord, give me strength.

"Maeve, the toilet is yucky and touching it can make you sick," I say, carefully choosing my words. "You need to come out and wash your hands."

"If the toilet's dirty," Emmie asks, "doesn't your butt get dirty when you sit on it?"

"Emmie just said butt!" Jack screams.

"Butt! Butt! Butt!" she responds, laughing hysterically.

"Here, put this on your butt," Jack says, flinging water at her backside.

"Maeve, come out of there now and wash your hands," I say with a rather shrill quality. She complies, but instead of unlocking the stall and walking out, she crawls out under the locked door on her hands and knees. She's now rubbed her hands all over the seat and the floor in front of a public toilet. I fight the gag reflex and forcibly lead her over to the sinks, where I would like to douse her in Lysol and instead scrub the living hell out of her fingers with the provided neon pink soap. Emmie and Jack are full-out splashing each other to the point where Emmie's shirt is wet and they are shrieking like I did at a New Kids On The Block concert, circa 1991. I channel my yoga breathing, in through the nose, out through the nose. I hear my instructor telling me to find my ujjayi breath, and focus on expanding my chest. If I pretend this isn't bothering me, it won't bother me, right?

Suddenly the door opens and a Chuck E. Cheese's employee stops dead in her tracks. Seeing it from her vantage point, I realize how out of control things have gotten. There's water all over the counters and the floor, almost an entire roll of paper toweling is unspooled on the floor, little pieces of which are tracked all over the tile. She widens her eyes and immediately backs out the door, probably summoning a manager. Although, this is Chuck E. Cheese's, and a destroyed bathroom is probably the least offensive thing she's seen. Adults were arrested and charged with disorderly conduct after a fight broke out this summer at this very same establishment. A couple of kids throwing water around aint' nothin'.

"All right," I say, leaning over and turning off the sinks. "I think that lady is going to send someone in here to yell at us. I need you to pick up the paper towels and wipe up the water on the floor so we can go play some more games. Isn't that why we're here?"

The kids settle down in the threat of real authority, aka a Chuck E. Cheese's manager, and clean up the mess. They dutifully file out of the bathroom and run screaming to the row of Skeeball machines. Jack starts whipping balls up the ramp like a boss, hitting the ten-thousand spot four times out of eight. He's a natural! Emmie, however, is not. She can't get the ball to roll up past the lip and throws herself on the ground crying about her lack of talent.

"Listen, Emmie, not everyone is good at everything," I say soothingly. "Well, except Mommy. But that's because I'm a grown-up and I have had lots of time to practice. Can I take a turn and show you what to do?"

"No!" she screams, flailing her arms and kicking her feet in classic fashion. If there was a video entry on Wikipedia for "tantrum," it would feature Emily. I start to laugh and she screams, "It's not funny!" While Screamy McScreamerson continues to put on a clinic about how to throw a tantrum, Maeve sidles up to the machine and grabs a ball. But instead of rolling it underhand like a normal person, she chucks it overhand like she's throwing from the mound at Wrigley Field. It bangs off the Plexiglass and bounces back at us, hitting Emmie in the head. This sets her off anew and I remark, "If you hadn't been throwing a tantrum on the floor, you wouldn't have gotten hit by the ball." There's always a teachable moment, isn't there?

I grab a token out of the cup and queue up my own set of Skeeballs. Jack is still zinging them in on my right like he's trying to qualify for the Olympic Skeeball team and his trail of tickets is pretty impressive. As I can't tell little Nolan Ryan to stop launching it overhand, I ignore her and instead inform Emmie, "Hey, there's no crying in Skeeball." I grab my first wooden sphere and heft the weight in my hand. I take a breath and roll it up: one thousand points. I could clearly use some work on my form. I grab the next and make it into the three thousand spot, which is much more acceptable.

Jack, meanwhile, has hit another ten thousand spot and I wonder if there is a scholarship in his future. I can see the *Sports Center* special now. "And with the first pick in the National Skeeball League draft, the Cyclones select … Jack Sprenger!" He'll be on Wheaties boxes, date a string of starlets, prevail in a minor performance-enhancing drug scandal and buy his parents a house in Hawaii. Josh will be so pleased when he hears we won't have to pay for college.

Maeve, however, should probably leave her Skeeball skills *off* any future resumes or college applications if this little show is any indication. She is still trying to perfect the rolling action, studying Jack intently. While she's now at least throwing it underhand, she's not successfully moving it more than a foot up the lane. I watch as she launches the brown ball over her shoulder and it rolls to the other end of the arcade. That could have been a lawsuit during a crowded weekend afternoon.

Emmie finally stands up and resumes her game, actually putting the ball in the hole. It's a miracle. She celebrates with a fist-pump and screams like she's the next contestant on *The Price Is Right*. Come on, act like you've been there before, Em. Don't embarrass yourself.

I post a respectable score of eleven thousand, but can't help laughing when I see how thoroughly Jack has schooled me – he's scored forty-six thousand points this round. The tickets pool around the bottom of the machine and his face is aglow with excitement. He grabs another token and quickly puts it in the machine and starts again. Maeve has abandoned all pretense of even trying to throw it underhand and instead climbs up onto the machine, walks gingerly down the lane to the Plexiglass and throws the ball under it. That's one way to do it. A bored employee stands nearby, sweeping something off the rug and doesn't even blink when she sees Maeve cheating. Apparently this sort of thing happens all the time.

After several consecutive games, Jack has racked up a serious amount of tickets. Too bad Chuck E. Cheese's tickets don't translate to cash. But then I guess it would be called a casino, not the Cheese. Emmie and Maeve have a handful each and I divide my strip equally among them, but they are still sorely lacking compared to Jack. But then he does something that makes me question whether aliens have kidnapped my child and replaced him without my knowledge.

"Mommy, I'm going to share my tickets with Emmie and Maeve so we can all get something together," he says magnanimously. I almost fall over from shock.

"Jack, that is very, very nice," I say, hugging his shoulders.

The kids skip ahead of me to the ticket-redemption machine and feed the strips of tickets in until we have a final count: three hundred and fifty-three. Jack grabs the ticket from the booth – he might be sharing, but he still wants everyone to know these are mostly *his* tickets – and they run to the counter to drool over the items they sadly have no chance in hell of "buying." The giant plush Chuck E. Cheese mouse is going for a cool one thousand tickets.

Fogging the glass case and smudging it with countless fingerprints, they wistfully inspect every last thing. Erasers, plastic vampire teeth, tattoos, jump ropes, Smarties, pencils, notebooks, bracelets, rings and fake colored hair extensions – nothing escapes their notice. Old enough to do the necessary math, Jack takes over the "do we have enough for" portion of the conversation and they scheme and barter with each other. They eventually bring home enough small, BPA-laden plastic toys to disrupt the hormones of a small country, which all break within thirty seconds. Except, of course, for the purple plastic kazoos, which will survive a direct nuclear hit. Those will still be going strong for weeks upon weeks.

Despite spending the morning inside, we still have plenty of time for outdoor activities after we get home. I grab the lunches I packed that morning and inform everyone we're going for a picnic. We manage to get to the park without incident and enjoy one of our better meals together. I don't care that they're spilling crumbs all over the blanket because it's easily shaken out and I care even less that they shriek and run around without finishing. They play an elaborate game of tag involving dinosaurs and princesses and I watch as they run around the sun-dappled grass. As we're leaving for home, Jack looks at me and says, "This was way more fun than camp, Mommy!"

He's right. Relaxing my rules and doing something different didn't result in death and destruction; instead, we had a great time throwing down at Skeeball. We're making memories, here, kids. Memories that set me back twenty bucks, but let's not quibble.

CHAPTER SIXTEEN
CANDYLAND ISN'T JUST A GAME ANYMORE

"Have you lost your mind?"

That's the response I've gotten from every single person who has asked what's new in our lives this month. Jack's teacher looked horrified, Emmie's teacher thought it was a great idea (she has a fifteen-month-old, she has no idea what's in store for her) and Maeve's teacher laughed and laughed and said she couldn't wait to see how it turned out.

My friends fear for my life.

"Wait, you're not going to say no?" my friend Jen asks. "To anything? My kids are not hanging out with your kids this month. I don't want to have to say yes by association."

My own babysitter, Sara, refused to work for us when she first heard the plan. But when I assured her that no, it was just me who had to adhere to the rules, she relaxed. "But I still think they're going to be terrors," she said. I didn't disagree with her. My sister-in-law, Marnie, went so far as to vacate to another state rather than have herself implicated in my nonsense. She disappeared to Arizona – in the middle of the summer, for god's sake – to get away from me and my yes mantra. My friend, Joanne, laughed and laughed when I told her of my plan. "Why the hell would you ever do that?" she asked. "Let me know when it's over so we can hang out again. That is, if they don't kill you first."

My friends, Vicki and Ally, sympathized with my plight, although they both said they find themselves saying "yes" willingly a lot of times.

"I say yes to a lot of stuff I shouldn't, but that's because I have working-mom guilt," Vicki said one night over drinks on a local wine-bar patio. "I feel bad I'm not with them, so when I am with them, I want it to be fun. I don't want to be the bad guy."

"The bad guy? For saying 'no, no you can not have ice cream for dinner?'" I ask.

"Well, I'm not that crazy. Oh, well, I mean, not that you're crazy …"

"No!" Ally interjected, laughing. "I mean you're not doing anything *really* crazy."

"Ally, I dropped hundreds of dollars on season passes at Six Flags, almost needed stitches in my lip and risked E. coli when my kids ingested ice out of a cooler at the store. The three of them have eaten their weight in ice cream each day, have forgotten what proper bedtimes are and now believe they can visit Chuck E. Cheese's on a whim. Oh, and I let Josh book two additional guys-only vacations, Emmie tattooed her face *and* her ass with ladybugs and my kids threw money at a homeless guy. I would say it's pretty much crazytown around here right now."

Ally and Vicki raise their glasses. "Cheers to the end of the month!" they laugh. Even my laid-back friends think this is nuts.

Out to dinner with Ian and Heidi one night, Ian asked why on earth I would willingly give up such crucial words.

"What's parenting good for if you can't say no?" he asked. "I don't get to say 'no' to my wife. I have to say 'no' to somebody."

When I first tell people about the plan, especially other moms, they act as if I have announced I am moving to Mars. There is shock, surprise and genuine confusion. And then the questions start. "Anything? They can do *anything* they want?" Inevitably the most-asked question comes up: "But what about food?"

My friends and family know I am a little extreme when it comes to the eating habits of my children. They eat only organic foods at home and they've never had a McDonalds Happy Meal. I don't say this to judge other moms or present our parenting as The Way To Do Things, but it's something we feel strongly about.

"So wait, what do they eat after school?" my friend Mandy asked one day, genuinely needing an answer.

"I don't know," I said. "Cheese sticks, fruit, carrots and hummus."

"Your kids do not eat carrots and hummus for a snack," she laughed. "You're lying."

"Bible," I said, holding up my right hand. "They totally do."

"Everything has transfats and high-fructose corn syrup in it, how do you even shop? Do you have a farm I don't know about?"

"That's the beauty of shopping exclusively at Trader Joe's and Whole Foods. They don't sell anything with crap in it, so I don't even have to think about it."

Mandy waved her hand dismissively. "I don't have time for that," she said. "If they don't sell it at Dominick's, it's not happening. My kids would revolt if I took away the high-fructose corn syrup and gave them an apple."

But that's the beauty of the friendships at our neighborhood school: you raise your kids your way, I raise mine my way, and we all go out for wine and complain about how hard it is. So when Mandy heard about my Yes Mommy plan, she laughed hysterically. "What are you going to do when they ask you for McDonalds? Or, god forbid, a Lunchable? Your kids are totally going to shove junk food in their faces all month and you won't be able to stop them!"

But for the most part, food hasn't been a big deal. Until now.

On the way home from soccer camp, I pull into the Wendy's drive-thru for a chicken sandwich for myself and Jack pipes up from the backseat.

"What are we doing?" he asks.

"I just need to grab some lunch for myself," I say, digging out my credit card. Let's be clear, the kids eat organic; I can still mainline transfats whenever I want, although I normally do it when they're not around. Driving through Wendy's with a kid in tow is uncharted territory.

"Can I have something? I'm starving."

I freeze. With every fiber of my being, I want to say no. Reflexively, I almost do. In any other circumstance, it would be out of the question. I stall for time.

"But I just bought turkey at Whole Foods to make sandwiches," I say. "Don't you want that?"

"No, I want Wendy's!"

"All right."

"Really? I can get something from here?" he asks excitedly. You would think I just offered him the chance to dine at Chicago's three-star Michelin restaurant, Alinea. Well, that would be my reaction to Alinea, not a seven-year-old's.

"Yes."

"Okay, I want a grilled chicken sandwich and a Caesar salad."

I almost drive into the screen depicting the twelve different value meals next to the drive-thru. If there is a god, he or she is surely shining down upon me. My child ordered a grilled chicken sandwich and a salad. My food lessons have made an impact; he really gets it!

Fast forward a few days.

"Mommy, is that our Halloween candy up there?" Jack asks one afternoon.

"Where?" I ask in a panic, knowing damn well what and where it is.

"Up there, in the cabinet."

I crane my neck and see a Ziploc bag peeking out of the top shelf with just a hint of a yellow wrapper showing in the corner. How he identified something I can barely see with a good foot of height on him is a mystery.

Here we go, I know what's coming next.

"Can we have some?" he asks.

"No," I say. "I mean, yes."

Old habits die hard.

I climb up on the two-step ladder, reach into the back of the cabinet and extract the bag. Emmie and Maeve appear at my feet, clamoring for their share. At no time did Jack alert them to the presence of said candy, they instinctively knew. They never just instinctively know it's bath time or that the toys need to be picked up, however. It's nice how that works.

The pack of wild dogs – I mean my children – swarm around me.

"Is that candy? Can we eat it? Please? I want some candy! I want M&Ms!" the throng of children is barking questions and requests at me, their little arms clinging to my legs, trying to climb up me. I'm Brad Pitt in a room full of single women – everybody wants a piece, but not of me, of the candy. I shake the children off my body and take a step back.

"Yes, you can have some candy," I say. "But you have to maintain some personal space and go sit down."

They immediately drop to their butts in reverent silence, hands in their laps, legs criss-cross-applesauce, as they call it. Their upturned faces smiling expectantly, Emmie squeals, "Can we pleeeeaaaasssseeeeee have some candy?"

I dump the whole gallon-sized Ziploc bag on the floor and they pounce. Elbows are flying and candy bars are being mushed into the floor inside their wrappers. Jack is unwrapping mini candy bars and eating them two bites at a time, then opening another and downing it, too. It's like some bizarre version of chain-smoking, but with Milky Ways.

Emmie opens a cherry heart-shaped sucker and takes a few licks, then quickly discards it so she can eat a package of Skittles. Maeve is methodically eating plain M&Ms one-by-one out of a fun-size pack, carefully inspecting each color before placing it in her mouth and chewing thoroughly. Someone knows how to savor her treats, although the big kids sense this is a once-in-a-lifetime opportunity and probably fear I will change my mind any second, so they shovel as much in as they can.

Jack is surrounded by a shredded pile of Twix and Kit Kat wrappers. He picks up a Snickers and asks me if it has peanut butter in it. I tell him no, just actual peanuts and he shrugs before ripping it open and taking a bite. He makes a face. "I don't like it," he says sadly. "Emmie, Emmie – here, try this. Look how many we have! You can have all of them." He gestures to a pile of ten fun-size Snickers bars and tries to push them toward her.

"No!" she screams. "I don't want those! Stop it!" her face is smeared with chocolate and sticky with juice from the cherry sucker. She stops chewing a pink Starburst and looks suspiciously at me. "Do we get to eat all this candy?"

"Yes, yes you do," I say, grabbing and unwrapping a Milky Way of my own. Maeve practically slaps my hand away and shrieks, "No, Mommy! That's ours! You can't have it!"

I raise my eyebrows at her as I sit back in our oversized chair, swinging my legs over the arm. "Oh really? Well guess what, yes I can." I pop the last bite in my mouth and lick the chocolate from my fingers. Yes Mommy, indeed.

Maeve throws herself on the ground, rolling over the candy, which destroys the piles Emmie was painstakingly sorting by type. Now the Snickers are mixed with the Skittles and the Smarties are piled on top of the Milk Duds and rogue pieces of Double Bubble are escaping to the side. Emmie immediately bursts into tears and starts shoving Maeve out of the way. When Maeve refuses to move, Emmie begins furiously kicking her in the back while screaming, "Get off my candy! Get off my candy!" Meanwhile, Jack is ignoring these shenanigans and steadily ingesting more and more candy. The pile of empty wrappers around him is impressive and he simply reaches under or around Maeve to get another piece.

Maeve finally stops rolling around in the candy long enough for me to hand her a fresh package of plain M&Ms, which she promptly opens and begins eating, tears still dripping down her pudgy cheeks. The chaos winds down and the children sit happily eating chocolate for a few minutes before Emmie loses interest.

"Mommy, I'm done," she says. All right, one down.

Maeve has abandoned her stash and wandered over to a nearby pile of LEGOs, where she is happily building something. Two down.

Jack, however, is two-fisting a Twizzler and a tiny box of Nerds while staring at the television, which has been a near-constant loop of PBS Kids since this whole Yes Mommy experiment started. I've lost control of the natives. But then again, did I ever really *have* control of the natives? His eyes are glazed over and I'm not entirely sure he's conscious. He moves his hand to his mouth to take another bite of candy, but that could just be reflexive. Perhaps I should check his pupil dilation and pulse.

The pile of uneaten candy grows smaller and the pile of wrappers seems to grow exponentially larger. I'm not sure how that's even possible. "Jack, are you done?" I ask, hoping the answer is in the affirmative, but not surprised when he shakes his head in the negative. I wander into the kitchen to see if the dinner fairy has made an appearance and am sadly disappointed to find she has not. There's a tooth fairy but not a dinner fairy? Being a grown-up is such bullshit. I gather the ingredients for spaghetti, setting a pot of water to boil and dumping a jar of marinara sauce in another pot. I have been known to make my own sauce on occasion, but this is not one of those occasions and Whole Foods does a fabulous job with its own version, so why recreate the wheel?

Thirty minutes later, dinner is ready and I ask Maeve to get the placemats and dishes out on the table. My request is met by silence, so I ask again over my shoulder while I plate the noodles and sauce. This time I hear a moan from a lump under a Hello Kitty blanket. All I see sticking out is a pale little face and a mess of blonde curls. "Maeve, come on, it's time to set the table," I say.

"No, Mommy, I can't," she whines. "My tummy hurts."

Oh teachable moments, how do I love thee? Let me count the ways.

"See? That's why we don't eat candy," I say without an ounce of sympathy. "It makes your tummy hurt. But too bad for you, you still have to come to the table for dinner. And please get out the placemats." Maeve cries, burying her head under the blanket and refusing to move. I notice Jack has a Pixy Stix dangling out of the side of his mouth as he watches *Wild Kratts*. Those enthusiastic nature-loving brothers would be very disappointed to see my child ingesting pure sugar with bonus food-coloring additives. You don't see Pixy Stix in the wild, although you normally don't see Pixy Stix in my house, either, so anything can happen. "Josh! Dinner!" I yell down the stairs to his office.

Emmie wanders over to the kitchen island, looks at the plates of spaghetti and announces, "I'm full."

"Too bad for you," I say. "But you're going to eat something besides candy for dinner. I don't care if you're full, a few bites of pasta and salad are a requirement. Jack and Maeve, please come to the table *now*!"

I quickly grab five placemats out of the armoire drawer and scatter them on the dining room table. Jack and Emmie carry their plates from the kitchen and I carry mine and Josh's. But Josh has also chosen to ignore me. I need a dinner bell.

"Jack, where is Daddy?" I ask. "Dinner is ready."

Jack shrugs his shoulders and picks up his fork. As I watch him chew a mouthful of noodles, I see Josh's head poke up at the top of the stairs. He stops and surveys Maeve lying on the couch, surrounded by the carnage of the candy explosion.

"What ... why ... where ... " he can't even form coherent thoughts. "What the heck happened in here?" Maeve starts crying, her face back outside the pink and yellow blanket again.

"Mommy said we could eat all the Halloween candy," Jack says, with slightly less enthusiasm than he had when this little escapade began.

Josh spins and looks at me. "You let them eat eight-month-old candy? That's disgusting. No wonder Maeve's crying. I would cry too if I bit into a rancid Kit Kat."

"It's not rancid, it's fine," I say. "Listen, that stuff has so many preservatives it could survive years in the cupboard. Besides, I'm not the one who held onto it. You put it in the top shelf of the cabinet where only you can see it. It was out of sight, out of mind as far as I was concerned.

Your son spotted it somehow, so really this is all on you."

Josh sits down at his spot and takes a long drink of water. I watch as Emmie pushes the pasta around on her plate and urge her to at least eat her spinach salad. If there's one thing I'm proud of as a mother, it's that my kids aren't picky eaters and are willing to eat a variety of healthy foods, including raw spinach and broccoli salads at dinner each night. But tonight, Emmie won't touch her salad with a ten-foot pole. Jack, however, is a growing boy and is robotically shoveling food into his mouth. When he's a teenager, we're going to go bankrupt trying to keep him in protein.

Maeve is still whining intermittently on the couch when we finish eating dinner. It's eighty-five degrees outside and the child is wrapped in a fleece blanket like she lives in an igloo. I step over the piles of wrappers that no one has bothered to throw in the garbage and sit down next to her. She's looking even paler than she did before. Alarmingly pale. In fact, I think she might—oh look, she's throwing up.

I yell for Josh to get a bucket as she heaves all over the rug in front of the couch. Thankfully, karma is not a bitch and the couch is spared. Jack and Emmie are in a tizzy, running from the living room to the kitchen and back. "Maeve threw up!" Emmie yells. Why thank you for that breaking news report. "Why does it smell like that?" Jack asks, pulling his T-shirt over his face. Well, let's have a discussion about stomach acid and digestion rates, but maybe not right now.

I start to strip the clothing off Maeve as she sobs and reaches for me. I feel bad holding her at arm's length, but the child is covered in puke. I try not to breathe as I carry her now-naked body up to the bathtub and leave Josh to deal with the situation downstairs. Shaking, with vomit in her curls, she sobs, "Mommy, I frew up. Mommy, I frew up." I know, sweetie, trust me, I know.

She screams as I put her in the tub and I calmly tell her I need to get her cleaned up. I wash and condition her hair and soap her from head to toe before rinsing her off and wrapping her in a hooded Hello Kitty towel. She's managed to calm down, save for sniffling and a few heaving gasps and I get her into some ladybug pajamas.

"Mommy, I frew up because I ate too much candy," she says with genuine remorse.

"I know, Maevie," I reassure. "But it's okay. Nobody is mad at you. Sometimes people just get sick and have to get the yucky stuff out of their tummies."

She sighs. "I am not eating any more candy." *Wanna bet*, I think.

I sit her in the upstairs hallway with an iPad and she happily amuses herself with *Plants vs. Zombies*. I unhappily walk back downstairs to assist with the cleaning. Josh is on his hands and knees scrubbing the carpet and I hear Jack and Emmie in the basement. I grab the bottle of Nature's Miracle (seriously, they should issue this to parents at the door of the hospital) and start spraying, trying not to gag. I've been a parent for seven years now and I still can't deal with the smell of puke. Of course, I'm wearing a tank top so I can't even pull it up over my face. I breathe in and out through my mouth and refuse to think about the smell.

Josh silently hands me the roll of paper towels and I blot as best I can without making eye contact. By rights, this should be all on me, but he's a trouper. We clean in silence for a few minutes and throw a towel over the wet spot so no one accidentally steps in the puke stain. Well, the stain formerly known as puke, now known as "the place Maeve threw up that one time" that looks just a shade off from the rest of the rug.

"I'm sorry," I say, not even making a snarky remark to go along with my apology.

"I know," he says.

Emmie emerges at the top of the steps and looks around. When she sees me, she bounces over and announces, "Mommy! We forgot to eat dessert! Can we have dessert?"

Seriously? I give up. Unlimited amounts of candy aren't enough? Not to mention this is the girl who didn't eat her dinner. Now she wants dessert? "You know what? Ask your father."

"Daddy, can we have dessert?" she whines.

"No," Josh says. "No, you may not."

I've never been so happy to hear those words in my life. Technically, it's probably cheating to pass it off on him, but I'm not cleaning up any more puke tonight, thank you very much.

CHAPTER SEVENTEEN
A FRIENDLY GAME OF CHICKEN

"I'm bored," Jack announces one hot, sticky morning. Bored? You have a house full of toys, iProducts of every sort, books, sporting goods and two different video gaming consoles. But apparently my spoiled special snowflakes need stimulation of some different sort.

"I wish I was bored," I reply. "In fact, there is nothing I wish for more in this life than to sit quietly on the couch and do nothing for hours."

"Why would you want to be bored?" he asks, genuinely confused. "I want to dooooooooooo something." He slithers from the top of the stairs all the way down to the living room, and lies in a little heap at the bottom of the staircase like a snake, coiled for a nap in the desert sun. Suddenly, he tenses, ready for attack. He pounces the two feet to the couch in a single movement, landing directly on Emmie, which sets her off. Pushing and shoving gets her nowhere, as he has a good twenty pounds on her, so she resorts to screaming directly in his ear.

No longer bored, he has resumed his most favorite activity in the world: annoying the living shit out of his sister. Poor Emmie was hanging out on the couch, kicking back with a little *Dinosaur Train* and suddenly, there's a terrorist suicide-jumping on her couch. Maeve waltzes up from the basement to see what's going on, clad in a Dora the Explorer dress-up skirt topped by a Captain America face mask. She takes one look at the scrum on the couch and goes right back downstairs. Smart girl.

"Boys and girls," I say loudly, "What is going on here?"

"Jack jumped on me … "

"Emmie is screaming in my … "

I ignore them both yelling simultaneously and put up my finger. No, not that finger. The "quiet right now" finger and they pause.

"Wanna go to Millennium Park?" I ask. The crowd erupts with whoops and cheers. Rock star mom, right here. Millennium Park is a cool park in downtown Chicago with huge fountains, an amazing mirrored sculpture called Cloudgate, which Chicagoans just call The Bean, an outdoor concert venue with an expansive lawn and sweeping views of both the Chicago skyline and Lake Michigan. It's a Chicago gem and one we try to visit a few times each summer. The fact we have to take the train there is a bonus for the kids. Not so much for the regular commuters, who probably don't appreciate the shoving and arguing over seats. Although come to think of it, that's typical of Chicago commuters themselves. Maybe the kids could teach them a thing or two about manners.

I tell everyone to get dressed so we can go, which means Emmie comes downstairs in her Fourth of July sundress, a beaded necklace and Tinker Bell charm bracelet completing her ensemble, and Maeve refuses to remove the Dora costume. I ask her if she's sure she wants to wear a purple polyester skirt and yellow polyester top over a pink sundress and she vigorously shakes her head in the affirmative. Alrighty then, Dora, let's explore Chicago! After the sunscreen gauntlet, the search for Mommy's flip-flops and Jack's insistence that he can unlock and relock our gate by himself, we're ready to go. Maeve insists that she can walk by herself without holding my hand, which prompts Emmie to sidle up to me and grab my left hand and smile at me. Such a pleaser, that middle child.

We walk the three blocks to the train with minimal complications, save for the usual brain aneurysm I have whenever Jack crosses the street without holding my hand. We arrive on the L platform and I start the usual chant of "Stay next to me. Stay away from the edge. Didn't you hear me? I said stay away from the edge. *Stay away from the edge!*" As Jack inches closer to the blue rubber strip demarcating the edge of the train platform, the Yes Mommy shit gets real and I abandon ship.

"Jack! No! Stop!" I yell as he steps firmly on the blue strip. Visions of my child electrocuted on the third rail and then run over by a brown-line train to the Loop flash through my mind and I yank him back toward the bench where the girls and I are sitting. This is one instance where I refuse to follow my own dictates – imagine the public outcry over the headline, "Mom lets son jump in front of moving train; says she couldn't say no because of stupid idea." Granted, that's way too long for even a three-column headline, but in the Internet age, anything is possible with these newfangled font sizes.

"What?" he says, shrugging my hands off his upper arm. "I wasn't doing anything, I was just looking for the train."

"I've told you hundreds of times that you can't be on the blue part," I say, calming down while releasing my shoulder blades out of the top of my skull.

111

The rest of my planned speech about being careful and listening to me so we stay safe is drowned out by the rumble of the train. Thankfully the rush hour is over, so we board a mostly empty car and the kids have their pick of seats. Of course, everyone has to sit by the window, so we take up the entire row of handicapped seating that faces outward. Listen, I'm handicapped by these three crazy people, but if anyone who actually needs the seats boards the train, I'll yank them out of there faster than you can say transit card.

The train picks up speed and the kids scream out landmarks they recognize from the neighborhood. Their faces are plastered so close to the windows that I'm not sure there is any longer a separation between the glass and their faces. They're laughing and talking animatedly about the passing scenery and I think of how I wish public transportation brought me this much joy. Maeve turns around in her seat, holding the metal pole for balance, and then absent-mindedly puts her fingers in her mouth. I run through the vaccination schedule in my head, determine she has never been inoculated against ebola and make a mental note to inquire about that at our next visit. In the meantime, I ask her to please not put her hands near her mouth and she responds by slowly licking her hand from palm to fingertips. Alrighty then.

I announce ours is the next stop and we should remain in our seats until the train comes to a complete stop. You can never be too careful with small, unbalanced people. This of course elicits the exact opposite response and all three children immediately stand up and topple over one another like dominos as the train comes to a stop. Sighing heavily, I help everyone stand up and carry a crying Maeve off the train and down the three hundred steps to the sidewalk. If there's one thing that annoys the living hell out of me about Chicago's mass transit, it's that more than half the city's train platforms are not handicapped-accessible. Annoying for me as a parent, life-altering for someone with a true disability who has no physical ability to visit swaths of downtown and the surrounding neighborhoods.

Maeve calms down and I am finally able to put her down an entire city block away, which does wonders for my back and shoulders. With renewed spring in my step, we head toward the fountains at Millennium Park with smiles on our faces. The kids immediately kick off their shoes, Maeve sheds her Dora costume and they take off running into the water, yelling and screaming as I helpfully yell, "Stay with your sisters!" at Jack. I gather our shoes and sit down on a bench, squishing in between a family talking animatedly in a foreign language over an open Chicago street map and a bored nanny, guarding a stroller with a sleeping baby who is oblivious to the nanny's rapid-fire Polish. At first I think she might be addressing me, but I realize she is wearing a Bluetooth headset and speaking into it, which is good because I don't speak Polish so that would have been a very short and very awkward conversation.

Normally I would admonish them to not run, but, you know, Yes Mommy and all, so I say nothing. Instead I resolve to let kids be kids and let the chips fall where they may. They may fall into the Lurie Children's Hospital waiting room, but hey, them's the breaks. And of course, it's not even ten minutes before we have our first injury of the day when Jack comes around the corner of the fountain at full speed and his feet slip out from under him. He goes down hard on his back and bounces his noggin off the tiled ground. I'm off the bench like a shot, kicking up water as I run toward him. He's my tough kid for sure, but he's already crying when I get there, sopping wet and trying to catch his breath while holding the back of his head. I can tell by the panicked look on his face that he's had the wind knocked out of him and he's struggling to breathe. If there's one thing I pride myself on, it's being good in a crisis. I sit him up, hugging his now sopping-wet body to mine. I lean him back from me and look him in the eye and instruct him to breathe.

He's gasping for breath as I'm telling him to calm down and take a deep breath. I can tell he's finally caught his breath when he lets out a blood-curdling scream. Anyone who thought I was his mother is now contemplating me as a child predator. He's crying, "My head hurts! My head hurts!" and I try to both hug him and assess the damage to the back of his skull at the same time. Emmie and Maeve are hovering close by, unsure of what to do. Maeve actually pats his back and says, "It's okay, Jackie," while Emmie helpfully asks if we need to call an ambulance. Jack clings to me as I convince him to stand up and come over to the bench with me. He's still crying and holding the back of his head, which is now erupting with an angry goose egg. There's no blood, which is a good sign, so we sit down on the bench and the girls run off holding hands as I yell, "Be careful! We don't need another injury!" They slow to a fast walk, which I consider one of my greatest parenting victories, right up there with teaching them about digital clocks and how they couldn't come out of their bedrooms until the first number was seven.

Jack sniffles next to me, burying his semi-wet head in my lap. At this point it doesn't matter as the entire front of my sundress is sticking to me. I thank the mothering gods it isn't a white dress, while I rub the back of Jack's head. He slows his sobs to sniffles and I gently ask him what happened.

"Well, I was running and I fell," he cries anew.

"You know what? This is exactly why Mommy always tells you not to run," I point out. I do love the teachable moments in life, especially during this little experiment. "Because when we run, people get hurt. Where are some places you should run?"

"Soccer?" he answers. "Gym class?"

"Those are good. Also, for money."

"What?"

"Never mind, Mommy was trying to be funny."

I hug him and he sits quietly for a few minutes, watching hundreds of people frolic in the two gigantic fountains, which are covered by two-story LED video screens. The screens show images of different faces and the water pours out of the mouths in the screens. It's a pretty amazing art installation in a city full of amazing art installations. The girls are pirouetting and spinning on the black tiles, which are covered in about two inches of water. They're wet and smiling and having the time of their lives. I ask Jack if he wants to join them and he shakes his head, he wants to eat lunch instead. I wave the girls over and ask if they're ready to go and the feet start stomping and the whining hits a feverish pitch. I say the magic words, "We can go out for lunch," and suddenly they're scrambling for shoes and telling me to hurry up and go. That's quite a change of attitude.

We start walking back towards the Brown Line and I somehow distract them to walk a little farther toward the Red Line, which will get us home slightly quicker. My plan is to hustle them down to the subway and take them to Chicago Bagel Authority when we get home. CBA does some amazing things with their bagel sandwiches, steaming them into cheesy melty goodness with soft surfaces and piping hot interiors. I highly recommend the DePaul Rueben if you're ever in the neighborhood. I'm dreaming of the corned beef and melted Swiss cheese when Emmie stops dead in her tracks on State Street and screams, "Mommy! Look!"

I follow her skinny finger and assume she's pointing at the giant Chicago Theater sign, the iconic symbol of our fair city, known all over the world. "Yes, Em, that's the Chicago Theater. That's where we saw *Yo Gabba Gabba*, do your remember?"

"No, Mommy, not that! Chick-fil-A! There's a Chick-fil-A!"

My blood runs cold and I plead with the universe that if time travel actually exists, that we could utilize it right now to go back in time and choose a different route home. One that doesn't involve the evil empire of Chick-fil-A and its delicious, delicious chicken and lemonade. You see, I have banned Chick-fil-A from our house for the last year after learning its Chief Operating Officer, Dan Cathy, donated millions of dollars to groups opposing LGBT rights and publicly made statements that he opposes gay marriage. I don't give a shit how good your chicken is, I will not allow my children to be brought up in a society where people are discriminated against for their sexual orientation and told they are not free to love whomever they want with the same legal rights as same-sex couples. I pretty rarely get on a soapbox about political things, but this is where I drew my personal line. I love me a fried chicken sandwich with that ridiculously awesome Chick-fil-A sauce, and their lemonade is like liquid crack, but it wasn't passing my lips ever again.

And the kids know of my stance. We drove past a Chick-fil-A on a road trip during spring break this year and they howled in protest when we drove right on by. Josh joined in the protest and asked, "Yeah, Mommy, why can't we have Chick-fil-A?" and I turned the radio down and gave them a kid-friendly explanation.

"You know how some people have a Mommy and a Daddy and some people have two Mommies and some people have two Daddies?" I began. "Well the man who owns Chick-fil-A doesn't think that men should be able to marry men and women should not be able to marry women. And in this family, we want everyone to be able to marry whomever he or she chooses. It's not nice for anyone to tell anyone else who they can love and it makes Mommy very sad that this man would be so mean to other human beings."

Ever understanding of complex situations, Emmie said, "Oh, I get it. So like I couldn't marry Maeve if we ate at Chick-fil-A." Ummm, that would probably be a question best posed to West Virginia legislators, and not really the sentiment I was trying to express. But hey, she kinda gets the concept, so we'll just keep working on it.

Josh was less enthused about my position telling me the highly conservative Koch brothers own a piece of practically everything I touch in my daily life. "If you're really going to take a stand and stop giving money to corporations that support anti-gay causes, then you better get out there and start using leaves to wipe your ass and stop driving or walking on asphalt, because they own it allllllllll, Amy."

Listen, I do what I can and my personal boycott of the chicken franchise makes me feel like I'm doing something to help the cause. But now, this direct request at a time when I absolutely can't say no might be the dagger to my heart.

"Oh, Emmie, don't you want to eat at the Potbelly's right across the street?" I practically beg.

"No, I want Chick-fil-A," she says. She begins chanting "Chick-fil-A! Chick-fil-A!" and gets Maeve and Jack to chime in. Passersby are laughing at the performance art we're staging in the middle of State Street during the lunch rush and I am sweating noticeably.

It is with a heavy heart that I escort the three of them to the glass doors and usher them inside. Emmie is smiling from ear to ear as we snake our way through to the front of the line. A chipper young man welcomes us to Chick-fil-A when we reach the counter and asks what we'll be having today. And at that moment the light bulb goes on in Jack's head and he looks at me in a panic. "Mommy, we're not supposed to eat here!" he yells. That's my boy.

The man at the register looks at Jack quizzically. "Why, do you have a food allergy of some sort?"

"No, Mommy says the man who owns Chick-fil-A doesn't like men getting married to men and that buying his food is bad," he says. I am so proud right now I could burst. The clerk has no idea what to say to this and looks helplessly at me.

"So, does he want a kid's meal or not?" he asks, the smile gone from his face.

I look at Jack and the lure of a free book and a chocolate shake with a cherry on top is too much for my budding civil-rights activist and he eagerly shakes his head in the affirmative, but asks for a side salad instead of the waffle fries. At least his food convictions are still going strong. I order kid's meals for the other two and emphatically tell him, "That'll be all."

"Nothing for you?" he asks.

"Not until gay marriage is legalized in every state of this nation," I respond from the tippy-top of my soapbox. I might have to let my kids eat the damn fowl, but it certainly won't pass my lips. I pay the bill and herd the children to the side to wait for the tray of food. Emmie and Maeve are chasing each other around my legs, screaming and laughing, but I'm oblivious to the stares of annoyance from the business people around us because I'm in a state of denial that this is even happening. Our order is ready and I balance the tray of food above the chaos of the children as we move toward a small table in the corner. I get everyone settled and negotiate the arguments over who gets the most strawberries out of the fruit cup and the one-thirtieth of a millimeter difference in the level of chocolate shake in the three different cups. Finally, everyone starts munching on his and her individual grilled chicken tenders and it's quiet until Maeve asks why I'm not eating.

"Because Mommy and Daddy don't think it's appropriate to eat at Chick-fil-A, remember?" I answer, ready for round two of educating my children on bigotry and big business.

"But Daddy has a sandwich when he takes us to Chick-fil-A," Emmie says.

"What? When does Daddy take you to Chick-fil-A?" I ask.

"After we go swimming with Mr. Matt and Lauren," Emmie says, licking Chick-fil-A sauce from her index finger.

"Yeah, Daddy says it's okay and that it's kind of like a surprise that we don't tell you about," Jack adds.

Busted.

"Does he? That is so interesting. I will have to thank Daddy for making that a surprise for me," I say.

I whip out my iPhone and text a picture of the kids posing with their meal bags, the Chick-fil-A logo front and center, captioned, "Kids asked to go to Chick-fil-A today for a secret lunch like they have with Daddy." I wait a few moments before the phone dings, alerting me to his response, which simply says, "Delicious." Whatever. I quickly reply, "You know where they don't have Chick-fil-A? Canada. Maybe we should move to Canada." He texts back, "You are not invited to Canada. I can always drive over the border to get it. I'm not worried."

The kids finish their meals and we leave the restaurant, walking toward the L stop. Emmie grabs my hand and looks at me nervously. "Mommy, are you sad?"

"Yes, I am a little sad, Em," I say truthfully. "I wish you guys hadn't chosen Chick-fil-A for lunch."

"I know, Mommy, but it was really good," she says, swinging my arm with hers. "Can we go there again tomorrow?"

Oh my god. I'm not going to make it to the end of the project because I'm going to be institutionalized.

CHAPTER EIGHTEEN
BEER ME

It's Saturday morning and I'm refilling my water bottle from the Pur dispenser in the fridge when Jack wanders over. I'm sweaty, but energized and he does a double-take. "Were you at yoga?" he asks.

"Yep," I say. As I'm wearing black yoga pants and a hot-pink workout tank, it was a pretty easy guess. This one is nothing if not observant.

"Oh." He holds the door to the fridge open and scans the contents. It's the same exact combination of items it was the last time he looked, which was a little more than an hour ago. I swear these kids think the grocery fairy just deposits things using a combination of magic and invisibility. They are constantly rummaging around for snacks or something to drink, wasting our precious energy and annoying their father, who has harsh words even for me when I leave the door open while I turn to grab a glass from the cabinet.

I gulp some water and put the blue Camelback bottle down on the counter. Jack picks it up and asks, "Is that water?"

"Yes, it is," I say absent-mindedly. "What did you think it was?" We don't drink soda or juice, so we don't keep them in the house. Literally the only thing in our fridge is milk, water, beer and half-empty bottles of wine. Although, let's face it, there's rarely leftover wine when I'm involved in the consumption.

"How come you don't drink beer?" he asks, gesturing to the drawer of bottles on the lower left side.

"Well, because after you work out, you need to drink water so your body gets healthy and strong," I say. "And beer is something grown-ups usually drink when they go out for dinner or something. Not usually right after they work out."

"Why not?"

"Well, it probably wouldn't taste very good right after I worked out and was trying to get hydrated."

"It tasted fine when I tried it."

A turntable-scratching moment commences.

"When did you taste beer?" I ask slowly, not wanting to make it seem like a big deal. Oh dear lord, we're going to have a little Drew Barrymore on our hands. He'll be coked out by twelve years old and headed to rehab. He'll be the kid who brings Jagermeister to the fifth-grade boy-girl parties and stashes Gatorade bottles full of vodka and juice in his school bag.

"Daddy gave me a taste when we were on vacation with Grandma Mary," he says innocently. "I didn't like it, actually."

"Well, that's interesting," I say. "But you know what, beer is for grown-ups only. So it really isn't a good idea for kids to drink it."

"Why not?"

"Well, it's actually against the law for kids to drink beer. And if a police officer sees you doing it, he might send you to kid jail." Jack is obsessed with jail tidbits, constantly asking what people do in jail, how old you have to be in jail, what happens if you die in jail – you know, your typical childhood daydreams. When I told him about juvie hall one day, his head almost exploded. Do they get to play outside? Do they go to school? Do they sleep there? Does anyone tuck them in? What about jobs? Do they have jobs? Every once in a while I slyly bring up kid jail and he ratchets the crazy down to more manageable levels. Genius.

"I'm going to kid jail?" he asks, going pale.

"No! Not at all. You were with Daddy and he said it was okay. Kids only go to jail if they drink a lot of beer and don't tell their moms and dads. Well, sometimes. Not always. Actually, no. Kids pretty much never go to jail for drinking beer. But you still shouldn't do it because it's not healthy. I mean not healthy for kids. Grown-ups are fine. Unless they drink too much and then they get sick."

Experts say one should never give more information than a child asks for. I am so far over that line right now, I fear I can't even see the horizon of the line any longer. I need to stop talking. Actually, I need to stop talking to Jack and start talking to his father, he who apparently gives beer to children. I send Jack outside with a garbage bag, gardening gloves and the promise of a dollar if he picks all the weeds growing alongside the house. He negotiates for two dollars and I quickly agree. Go forth, young man, and eradicate the future clover patches.

I stand at the entrance to the living room, leaning against the black marble façade of our two-sided fireplace. The fireplace we thought would be so amazing and cool, but ended up using twice in seven years because the gas smell is so noxious when it's in use. I lean and wait for Josh to look up from his laptop at me. I wait and wait and wait some more. I clear my throat and he looks up.

"What?" he asks.

"What?" I repeat.

"Do you need something?" he replies.

"Do I need something?" I ask, mimicking him snottily. "Yes, as a matter of fact, I do need something. I need to know what were you thinking when you gave our seven-year-old a beer!" I genuinely believe at this moment that he has lost his damn mind. Maybe he had a stroke or some sort of break with reality.

"I didn't give him a beer, first of all. It was a sip. One sip."

"Sir, please let the record reflect the witness has admitted to giving the child beer."

"There is no one else here. It's just us. No one is taking dictation on testimony. Calm down, for god's sake. It's so not a big deal. You get to say yes to whatever you want, how come I can't?"

"Because I would break the damn rules of the deal if my seven-year-old son asked for *beer*."

"You're being insane," Josh says. "First, it was one sip. Second, he didn't like it. Third, I'm about to totally blow your mind. Are you sure you're ready?"

"Just say it already."

"What I did is perfectly legal in the great state of Wisconsin."

"No, it's not," I reply, getting even more annoyed. Now he's trying to lie about liquor laws.

"See? Your mind has been blown." Josh whips open his laptop and starts reading. "Here you go: 'The drinking age in Wisconsin is twenty-one. Those under the legal drinking age may be served, possess, and/or consume alcohol if they are with a parent, legal guardian, or spouse who is of legal drinking age.' Is that not the craziest thing you've ever heard?"

"Where are you reading that?"

"Wikipedia."

"Wikipedia? Anybody can edit that. You just wrote that in there."

"Wikipedia is like the Bible, honey. It can't be questioned. It's rock solid."

I take a deep breath. "Josh, you can not give children beer, despite what the state statutes say. Even in Wisconsin."

"Listen, there is actual photographic evidence of you drinking from a beer bottle when you were two years old," Josh counters. "And you grew up in Wisconsin! It was in our wedding slideshow for god's sake. And you're bitching at me about letting Jack have a sip of beer? Pot, please meet kettle."

"First of all, I am neither the pot nor the kettle. That would, in fact, be my father, who let that happen. Second of all, it was the 1970s. Moms still smoked and drank when they were pregnant. I think every kid our age has a picture exactly like that. Parents were a lot more laid-back then."

"Exactly! You are way too uptight. I thought this Yes Mommy thing was all about you relaxing and not having a coronary over every little thing."

"Yes, yes it was. But we agreed: no tattoos, no smoking and nothing dangerous."

"It's Labatt Blue, not crack, Amy!"

"So bizarro-world Canadian Josh gives his kid Canadian beer and it's okay?"

"I will not have you referring to my love of Canada as bizarre. It's a deep and abiding love, pure like a glacier snow."

"Glacier snow is subject to air pollution just like all the dirty sewer snow in Chicago. Stop acting like it's unicorn snow or something."

"I'm not going to stand here and let you denigrate the great country of Canada. The snow there is unblemished and pristine. I am offended you feel the need to attack it. You're clearly feeling inferior as an American."

"Oh my god! You're an American, too!"

"I'm converting," he says. "Just like people convert to Judaism. But there's no classes and I don't have to learn to read another language backward."

He's lost his mind. Gone. I need to file a missing persons report for his brain. "This has nothing to do with snow!" I take a deep breath and calm myself. I think about my yoga practice and try to center my breathing for a moment. "Josh, you gave our son beer. Do you want Child Protective Services at the door?"

Josh throws his hands up in the air, exasperated. "You're being insane. First, he asked for it, I didn't give it to him. Second, it was one sip. Third, he didn't like it. Fourth, they serve Labatt's to children in Canada all the time. It's no big deal."

"They serve beer to children in Canada?" I ask incredulously.

"Well, I assume it's like France. French people don't have ridiculous hang-ups about alcohol like Americans do."

"Listen, we're not in France or Canada; we're in the United States of America and the drinking age here is twenty-one. Last time I checked, Jack is not twenty-one, he's seven."

"You're saying you never had a sip of beer before you turned twenty-one? Because I just told you I have photographic evidence that you did."

I hold my hand up. Enough.

"Can you just please promise me you won't give him any more beer?"

"Like ever? Even after he turns twenty-one, because that's just stupid."

"Can we please not do this right now? You know what I mean. I have enough problems with these children this month without you giving them beer. Please."

Josh sighs and mutters something under his breath as he walks away. I really don't want to fight with him right now – my sanity is hanging on by a thread and I need him to stay with the kids so I can get a pedicure. I jump on his back horsey-back style and wrap my arms around his neck, kissing him on the side of the face.

"Hey! What the—get off me, you're killing my back!" he says in surprise.

"Listen, let's be lovers, not fighters," I say.

"You want to be lovers right now? The kids are playing Wii downstairs, we could totally sneak upstairs … " He grabs my hands, separating them so I slither to the ground behind him. He turns and offers me his hand and pulls me up into an embrace.

"Don't be absurd. I need a pedicure and you're the lucky winner of the 'Who Gets To Stay With The Kids' sweepstakes." I put my hands around his neck and kiss him fifteen times on the cheek making that annoying "mwah" sound each time and he literally runs away from me to the other side of the house to get away from my onslaught of schmoopie.

The word "pedicure" is still hanging in the air when Emmie sticks her head around the wall at the top of the stairs and asks with a hopeful smile, "Mommy, can I come, too?"

Well, there goes my relaxing pedicure with the latest copy of *Us Weekly*.

"Sure," I say, "come on."

As we walk across the street to the nail shop, Emmie is practically levitating. She talks a mile a minute about how excited she is. She barely has enough to time to tell me what color nail polish she's going to get before we're at the entrance to the nail shop. We walk down the stairs to the entrance and her face lights up when she's greeted by rows upon rows of OPI polish. My girl can swing a bat with the best of 'em and routinely whips boys' asses in coed soccer, but she loves her some pink glittery nail polish on her toes while she's doing it.

"Oh, Mommy! Look at all the colors!" she exclaims. "Can I get my hands and my toes?"

Knock yourself out, it's Daddy's money! She carefully chooses a pink glittery polish for her fingers and a purple glittery polish for her toes and settles down into a chair. I pick my own boring pale pink for my fingers and magenta for my toes and sit down in the adjoining chair, snapping photos of my five-year-old literally being waited on hand and foot by a woman four times her age. Shameful.

Emmie keeps glancing at me as if to reassure herself that this is actually happening, that I allowed her to finally get a real mani-pedi. I smile and ask if she's having a good time and she nods vehemently in the affirmative.

Sure, the fumes alone probably took five years off her lung function and her future reproductive years could be questionable after the chemicals leach into her bloodstream, but she's having fun.

She chatters about an episode of *Phineas and Ferb* she watched that morning, some nonsense that I didn't actually follow about a platypus, and I nod and smile. She switches topics quickly to ask what we're having for dinner and then leans back and sighs.

"Mommy, this is so awesome," she says dreamily.

Normally, I would be annoyed that the person next to me was interrupting my "me" time. I like my pedicures silent, except for the splashing of the foot tub and the rustle of my magazine pages turning. But this is a whole different experience. I'm actually enjoying myself, laughing with Emmie when she says something funny and realizing she's not such a little girl anymore. As we switch to the manicure station, I watch as she sits perfectly still and quiet, almost daring not to breathe. Unlike her brother, this one is able to sit without fidgeting, without constant motion, without twenty-four-seven stimulation. She's happy to sit with a book for a half-hour on the couch or play quietly with her American Girl doll. And the ability to chill out makes her the perfect candidate for a girly day out in the future.

We let our nails dry under the lamp for a bit, not talking. As we walk up the stairs to the street, Emmie throws her arms around me. "Thank you, Mommy!" she says.

"No, thank you, Emmie," I say, hugging her back and truly not caring if I smudge a nail in the process. "This was so much fun. I'm glad you came along."

That night, looking back, I realize the old mommy would have said nope, this pedicure time is mine and I earned it. But I would have missed out on some pretty amazing mother-daughter bonding time. Someday, in the not-too-distant future, she's going to want nothing to do with me. Pedicures will be time spent with her friends, although I'm sure she'll have her hand out for the cash to have it done. My time with my daughter is precious and I need to make the most of it. The beer debacle, too, seems much less critical in hindsight. It was one sip and Josh was most likely trying to be funny. I know he wasn't sending our son down the road to alcoholism with the dregs of a Canadian beer. It wasn't a drag off a cigarette for god's sake. This month is about lightening up a little and letting the kids make their own mistakes. Maybe that goes for Josh, too. I don't always have to micromanage his parenting, swooping in when I don't like or agree with his choices. He has just as much say around here as I do.

I wander downstairs and plop down next to him on the couch.

"Hey, sorry about my reaction to the beer thing," I say sincerely.

He looks over his shoulder and back at me. "Are you addressing me?"

he asks wryly. He acts like I never apologize.

"Well, my boyfriend isn't allowed in the house when you're in town, so yes, I'm talking to you," I say.

"Then I accept your apology. Does this mean next time I can split the can with him?"

I open my mouth to screech and he laughs. "I'm kidding! I just wanted to see what you would say. I promise you, he didn't like it and I won't be offering again. I just wanted a little taste of Yes Daddy for a few minutes."

"You're more than welcome to your own month of Yes Daddy. In fact, it would be a great sequel to *Yes Mommy*!"

"No no no, I'm not writing *Yes Daddy*. I have much bigger plans. *Fifty Shades of Daddy*. It's going to sell gangbusters. In fact, I think we should start researching that right now."

I laugh and pull back from his kiss. "Listen, that ship has sailed. You're about a year too late. Although I'm sure there's an untapped market for daddy porn, it's not what you think. For most women, daddy porn would be a tale of a man who does the laundry, gets up with the kids every morning, cooks and cleans and suggests Mommy goes on girls weekends once a month."

Josh scoffs. "No one wants to read a non-fiction account of our marriage, Amy."

CHAPTER NINETEEN
THE DAY OF RECKONING

"What's for dinner?" Jack asks, sliding sideways into the kitchen on the hardwood floors.

"Mrs. Dean's Dish," I say, stirring the ground beef that I am browning on the stove.

"Who's Mrs. Dean?" he asks.

"A friend of my grandma's," I say, giving the boiling egg noodles a quick stir. "She put this recipe in a cookbook and my grandma made it for Grandma Mary when she was a little girl and Grandma Mary used to make it for me and Auntie Beth when we were little and now I'm making it for you and your sisters while you're little."

Mrs. Dean's Dish is simply ground beef, egg noodles and cream of chicken soup mixed together as a casserole, seasoned with a little garlic powder and salt and pepper. It's easy and something my kids love, which makes it part of the regular rotation.

Jack runs upstairs screaming, "We're having Mrs. Dean's Dish!" but I can't hear the response because the thundering herd of elephants above my head drowns everything else out. I quickly drain the noodles and add them to the ground beef and cream of chicken soup and turn the flame down to a simmer.

Maeve appears next to me out of nowhere and asks what we're having for dinner. I tell her Mrs. Dean's Dish and she bursts into tears. "I don't wanna have Mrs. Dean's Dish," she sobs. "I want Daddy's chicken wings."

Josh recently discovered the best chicken wing recipe in the history of chicken wing recipes and we're all obsessed with eating the wings he makes on the gas grill. But unfortunately, Daddy is the maker of the chicken wings and even if I could whip up a batch, the wings need to marinate for a

125

minimum of three hours and take fifty minutes to grill. We're dangerously close to the witching hour here and I need to get some food in these children before they revolt.

"Maevie, I want Daddy's chicken wings, too, but he's not home so there's no one to make them," I say, trying to soothe her.

"I want Daddy!"

"I want Daddy, too. Trust me, there is no one here who wishes Daddy wasn't traveling for work more than your poor, overworked, exhausted mother."

"I want some milk!"

"What do you say?"

"I want some milk *now.*"

I walk into the living room. I don't care if I'm not allowed to say no, I will not be addressed so rudely. Maeve follows me with her purple sippy cup, waving it in my face. "I want milk!" she screams at me.

I pick up a copy of *Chicago Magazine* that recently arrived and flip through it. I do not negotiate with terrorists. The terrorist tyke in question responds by grabbing the magazine out of my hand and throwing it on the floor.

"Hey! That is not nice," I yell.

"Milk!" she screams at me. For emphasis, she throws the empty sippy cup at my head with deadly accurate aim. *That did not just happen*, I think to myself, *I am hallucinating.*

"Did you just throw that at me?" I ask rhetorically. "You are going for a timeout."

I might not be able to say no, but I can damn well put this child in her room for three minutes. I tell her to go upstairs and shockingly, she does not respond immediately by walking up the stairs. Instead, she stamps her foot and crosses her arms. In response, I pick her up and carry her to her room. She's flailing and bucking like a bronco, but I manage to plop her down in her room and shut the door with minimal injury to myself. I do end up with a broken nail, but I consider that a success. I walk down the hall to the bathroom and stare at my reflection in the mirror. The dark circles under my eyes are hideous; it looks like someone punched me in the face. I grab a pot of Benefit Erase Paste out of my makeup bag and set to making them look less heroin-chic when I hear a thud. I pause and it's followed by a bang. What the hell is going on back there?

I quickly walk back to Maeve's room and I hear another loud bang from the doorway. I open the door to find the wooden pieces of her puzzle stool scattered on the floor in front of the door, the six-inch tall "A" in her hand, cocked behind her head. When she sees me throw the door open, she stops, then continues on and launches the wooden piece at my chest, where it connects and falls to the floor.

"What are you doing?!" I scream at the top of my lungs.

In response, she turns and picks up the stool, now emptied of its pieces, and lifts it over her head. I swoop down and grab it before she can throw it at me and I get right down in her face.

Before I can even think, I scream, "No!" I continue, like a woman possessed. "No no no no no no no!" I grab her hands and look her right in the eye and yell it again for good measure. I'm shaking and she starts to cry. Even without violating the basic rules of the month, it would not have been my finest parenting hour. But I'm even more of a failure because of that. I stand up and walk out of the room, turning my back on my crying child. I need to walk away right now before I say – or do – anything worse.

I go downstairs, shut the flame off under the pan and wordlessly spoon the casserole onto three plates. I pour everyone a glass of milk and put everything on the table. I yell, "Dinner's ready" and stand at the kitchen island, checking my e-mail on my laptop. Maeve walks slowly by me, sniffling and wiping her eyes, and the big kids quietly come down from upstairs where they were playing on the computer during the screaming incident. They warily sit down and start eating but then Emmie chooses the wrong time to complain.

"This doesn't taste good," she says with disgust.

I whip around and hiss, "You know what? Then don't eat it. I don't care."

"Can I have grilled cheese instead?" Emmie whines.

I explode.

"No! No you can not have grilled cheese," I yell. I'm on a roll.

"Why are you yelling at me?" Emmie asks, bursting into tears. Clearly she's gotten used to the Yes Mommy treatment these last few weeks.

I look at my sobbing daughter, tears dripping onto her uneaten food and I head for the bathroom. I lock the door behind me and sit down on the closed toilet seat, my face in my hands. I can't do this anymore. It's not possible. I can't allow them to do whatever they want and say whatever they want and eat whatever they want without repercussions. I've tried, I've really given it a go. But this isn't normal. No mother is capable of saying yes all the time.

What have I done? My kids are turning into spoiled brats who have the world on a string. I've lost control, and more important, I've lost the will to continue this project. And I just ruined it anyway by screaming "no" at my tired, hungry three-year-old. Jack knocks on the door and says he has to pee, but I tell him to go upstairs. I sit perfectly still for several minutes, ignoring the arguing over who has more milk in her cup. A few minutes later I hear the house phone ring and Jack jumps up to answer it.

"Hi Daddy," I hear through the door.

"Eating dinner," he says, before putting the call on speaker.

"What are you having?" I hear Josh ask.

"Mrs. Dean's Dish," Jack responds.

They chat for a few minutes before I hear Josh ask, "Where's Mommy?"

"Well, she's in the bathroom," Jack says. "She yelled at Emmie and then she went in there and she won't come out."

"What?" Josh asks.

"I said she yelled at Emmie and now she won't come out of the bathroom."

"Take the phone to the bathroom door." Jack knocks on the door and announces Daddy is on the phone.

"Tell him I don't want to talk to him," I say through the door.

"Daddy, she doesn't want to talk to you."

"What? You tell her she is lying to herself. She always wants to talk to me. She looks forward to nothing more in her life."

"Mommy, Daddy says you're lying. He says you always want to talk to him."

"Tell him not always."

"Daddy, she says not always."

"Then ask her why she calls me ten times a day when I'm trying to work."

"Mommy, he says then why do you call him ten times a day at work?"

"Tell him those must be wrong numbers I was dialing."

"Daddy, those were wrong numbers."

"Is she seriously not going to talk to me?"

"Mommy, are you really not going to talk to him?"

I begrudgingly open the door wide enough for him to pass the phone in and then I shut it again.

"Are you seriously hiding from the children?" Josh asks incredulously.

"Yes," I snap back.

"You're being ridiculous," he says. "How old are you? Do I need to hire a babysitter for you *and* the kids now? Knock it off."

"I am *not* being ridiculous," I say, starting to cry. "Maeve threw things at me not once, but twice tonight. I screamed at her – and said no like a million times – before I did the same with Emmie after she said dinner was gross. I'm out. I can't do this. You need to come home."

Josh softens his tone. "You know I can't fly home. What is going on? You need to calm down and take a deep breath."

"No, what I need to do is give up on this project. It's killing me. I just can't anymore. It's killing me – the nonstop gratification, the swallowing of my discipline, for god's sake I let them eat at Chick-fil-A! I compromised my beliefs!"

"I truly don't think your fifteen-dollar tab is solely responsible for keeping gay marriage off the books in Alabama," Josh says soothingly. "And if you really think it's ruining the kids, then stop. But look how close you are. And think about all the things you've done so far that has brought them joy and hasn't killed you. All the times you've let them eat ice cream and candy and didn't tell them to stop playing outside in the rain or get mad when they stayed up late giggling. And letting me book that trip to Mexico – that was pretty amazing."

I sniffle. "I still can't believe I let you do that. I'm so stupid."

"Listen, it's going to be fine. You're in the homestretch. You can see the finish line. Take it one game at a time. Be the yes."

"What does that even mean?" I ask.

"I have no idea, I was going for a metaphor like 'be the ball.' That's all I got. I'll be home tomorrow. Just get yourself together. And if you're going to stay in there, at least do something useful and clean the toilet."

I laugh before hanging up and look down to see four little fingers wiggling at me under the door. I hear Maeve whisper, "Mommy? Mommy, are you in der? I sorry Mommy."

I open the door and hug her.

"Mommy's sorry, too," I say while rubbing her back. "I'm sorry I yelled at you."

Maeve lays her head on my shoulder and asks in a quiet voice, "Can I have some milk please?" If she had just asked this nicely in the first place, we could have avoided all of this.

I declare a shower-free night and put the kids to bed with minimal fuss. I apologize to everyone when I tuck each of them in and Emmie asks why am I sorry. Apparently she has amnesia when it comes to my parenting shortcomings, which could come in very handy someday. I explain to her that even mommies have bad days and that I will try harder tomorrow. She hugs me fiercely and tells me her wish for tomorrow is that we can have a better day. Mine, too, Em, mine, too. That's the beauty of this parenting thing: you always get a fresh start in the morning.

I walk downstairs feeling like shit and pour myself a glass of wine. I sit on the front porch steps, the front door cracked open behind me, swirling my Pinot Noir and replaying the events of the evening, realizing I brought it on myself. Every time I have failed in this, it's been because I tried to push back and not act in the spirit of the project. If I had just sucked it up and gotten Maeve some milk, the chain of events could have been avoided. Just like when I wouldn't let her ride in Beth's car and I got a fat lip because of it. I just need to recommit. And remember that it's almost over. I am Yes Mommy; hear me roar.

CHAPTER TWENTY
IN THE HOMESTRETCH

I've hit the point where I am so sick of this project I just can't see the end of the tunnel. I want to stay home, hide in my bedroom and eat cookies all day. Just the thought of taking the children out in public makes me want to weep. I'm exhausted, my tongue has permanent indentations where I have to bite it to keep quiet and I have developed an eyelid twitch.

The kids, however, are loving life. Food restrictions? Gone. Sleep patterns? Disrupted. Clothing choices? Questionable. Screen time? Unlimited. They're in danger of going feral. Their father, ever helpful due to his travel schedule, is also living it up.

My cell phone rings one morning and Josh's picture pops up on the screen. I slide the green bar to answer the call and greet him with a bored, "Hey." We're very romantic.

"So, guess where I am?" he yells into the phone.

"Michigan? Because that's where you better be, considering you told me that's where you would be when you left on Sunday night," I reply.

"Nope. Guess again."

"What do you mean, 'nope'? You're supposed to be in Michigan."

"I've realized my dream, it's all come true. I'm here, in the Promised Land."

"You're in Israel?"

"I'm in Canada!" His sounds positively giddy.

"You are not," I say. "Knock it off."

"No, I really am. I realized that Canada is a mere bridge-crossing away from Detroit. So here I am. It's exactly how I pictured it. It's amazing!"

"Josh, please know that Windsor looks exactly like Detroit. They're like five hundred feet apart. I could throw a baseball from Detroit to Windsor. I

130

doubt it looks or feels any different."

"Are you kidding? It's totally different!"

"Oh right, I forgot. Windsor has casinos and strip clubs. Detroit has, well, I'm not sure Detroit-proper even exists anymore. Didn't everyone move out of downtown when they declared bankruptcy? Did they all move to Eight Mile with Eminem?"

"*Fully nude strip clubs*, Amy. I just want to point that out."

"And how do you know this?"

"Everyone knows that. It's in the handbook they issue you when you cross the border."

"Speaking of crossing the border, my dear Joshie, how exactly did you do that without a passport?"

"Oh, I have it with me. I remembered to grab it before I left this week."

"So this was a premeditated trip to Canada?"

"Aren't they all? You don't just swear allegiance to the queen on a whim."

"I don't think you had to swear allegiance to the queen to get in. Just to become a citizen. Which you didn't do, did you? Oh dear god, please tell me that you haven't taken it that far."

"Don't be ridiculous. Of course I didn't emigrate."

"You did this just to prove a point, didn't you" I ask exasperatedly.

"Duh. I always win, Amy. Now, I bid you a fond au revoir."

"Umm, Josh? You know they only speak French in Quebec."

"Whatever. I'm just practicing for my next trip to Montreal. You know, when we use our season passes at Six Flags LaRonde."

"Enjoy your time in the great north," I say, laughing. "Get some free health care while you're there. Oh, and bring me some Tim Horton's! I love their doughnuts."

"I wish you were here," he says. "Seriously. It's not nearly as funny without you to witness my one shining moment."

"I'm happy for you. Really. Now get your ass back on American soil. And don't forget my doughnuts."

Their father is realizing his life-long dream of rolling around in Canadian soil and the children and I are still slogging through on the home front. While they're having a grand time as individuals as the project comes to a close, they're not so homogenous as a sibling unit anymore. Not that they ever were, but at least I kept major wars in check. That's a thing of the past, however.

Later that same afternoon they ask to play outside, so we schlep the baseball bats and soccer balls and bicycles and snacks and sunscreen to a nearby school that features blacktop, a turf soccer field and playground equipment. Everybody's happy – and hot. It's approximately eleven thousand degrees in the sun and the only shade to be found is a postage-stamp sized area already occupied by some random chick reading a book and eating out of a brown paper bag. Sister, you are really going to regret your choice of locale once these kids start screaming. Perhaps a nice bench near the Oz Park gardens a few blocks down would be a better choice.

The big kids are tearing in circles on their bikes on the blacktop and Maeve is furiously peddling her tricycle as fast as her little legs will pump, but can't keep up. This causes her to release some sort of combination primal scream and grunt. This is what I imagine Big Foot sounds like. I wipe the sweat from my forehead and yell over to her.

"Do you want some help?" I ask.

"No!" she responds in her outside voice to me, then screams at her sister, "Emmie! Wait for me!" Emmie, of course, ignores her, which sends her into some sort of transformative fit. Her face contorts and I'm pretty sure she turned green and ripped off her shirt. Maeve tries to push her tricycle down in a fit of anger, but its stability confounds her and she ends up falling over it as she shakes it. Now she's really screaming and as I reach her, she pushes me away. "I can do it myself," she screams. Well, that hasn't worked out so well for you up to this point, sweetie, but I back off and leave her be.

I turn my back on Toddler Incredible Hulk to see Jack off his bike, running alongside Emmie, trying to grab her handlebars. Of course my first instinct is to yell, "No!" Instead I observe as Emmie falls off the side of the bike in slow motion and crumples in a heap. I'm over there like a flash, picking her up and simultaneously hugging her, wiping her tears and assessing the damage. Her knees are both skinned and bleeding, as is the side of her right hand and her right forearm. When she sees the blood, she starts hysterically screaming, "I need a band-age! I need a band-age!" She still doesn't pronounce it correctly and I might never correct her because it's so adorable.

Soothing her, I turn on Jack. "What was that for?" I ask, eyes flashing anger.

"I wanted her to come on the climbing thing with me and she wouldn't get off her bike," he shrugs.

"So you just threw her off her bike to get her to play with you?" I ask. The thought process of the seven-year-old is both mystifying and nonsensical. "You do realize she's not going to play anything with you now because she's bleeding?"

"She's bleeding?" Maeve sticks her bike-helmeted-head three inches from Emmie's wounds. "Oooo, Emmie, you need a band-age!" She pokes at one of Emmie's knees for confirmation it is actually blood, which causes Emmie to haul off and knee Maeve in the face. This throws Maeve off balance and as she tries to break her fall with her hands, they slide across the asphalt, losing a layer of skin in the process. Now Maeve is both crying and bleeding as well.

I abandon Emmie to pick up Maeve and hug her, which leaves Emmie free to exact her revenge on Jack, which she quickly does. Despite her bloody knees, she quickly pounces at him and he tries to escape, but the tangle of bikes and bodies prevents a clear escape route and he trips over one of Emmie's training wheels, sprawling himself prostrate on the ground. His scream takes a second to gain traction, like it did when he was an infant, but once it does, no one misses it. I'm pretty sure they heard him at Lurie Children's Hospital downtown and are now readying the chopper for an airlift. I'm afraid to look at his face for fear he's knocked out several teeth and wonder exactly what our lifetime dental insurance coverage amounts to.

I set Maeve aside to tend to the newest injury, turning him over and helping him up. His teeth – at least the ones that are supposed to be there – are all still in place, but his poor little cheek is pockmarked by road rash and bits of gravel. Jack is my kid with the highest pain tolerance I have ever seen, but once he's actually *in* pain, it's tough to calm him down. Typical man. His keening is likely disrupting satellite transmissions in other countries, and certainly doing damage to my delicate ear mechanisms.

"Emmie did this to me!" he screams, collapsing into my left side. I hug him and rub his hair, rocking him like when he was a baby. Emmie tries to push him out of the way, and he kicks out at her, so she snuggles into my right aide and I kiss her hand. Not to be outdone, Maeve dives between them and shoves her way onto the middle of my lap. All three kids are crying – and still wearing bike helmets. I barely keep my face out of the way of their molded black and pink plastic orbs as they jockey for position in my embrace. Maeve is kicking both Jack and Emmie in her quest to oust them from their spots and both of them are trying to shoulder her closer to the other one's side. As Maeve pushes back, she knocks her Dora helmet square into my cheek and I see stars.

"Guys!" I say, raising my voice. "Enough!"

I dump everyone off my lap and stand up, pressing fingers into my cheekbone, wondering how fast the bruise will show up and whether people will really believe me when I tell them that no, Josh doesn't beat me.

All four of us now have tears in our eyes and I press my fingers to the bridge of my nose to buy myself a minute – and to dull the pain in my cheekbone. "Come on, we're leaving," I say after a moment.

"No! We don't want to leave!" they cry in unison.

"I'm sorry, what? You're all lying on the ground in various stages of triage, kicking and shoving each other. It certainly doesn't look like you're having anything resembling a good time. No one is being nice to anyone else. No one is playing nicely together. No one is smiling. Get the stuff, we're going home."

"No, we'll be nice!" Jack cries. "Please! Emmie, Emmie, do you want to play something? Let's play something."

Loathe to make up with her tormentor, but more loathe to leave the park, Emmie stands up and agrees to play with him. They abandon the bikes and limp off toward the playground equipment. Maeve turns her back on both of them and asks for my iPhone. At least she doesn't suffer from Stockholm Syndrome like her sister.

I lead Maeve over to the shady bench – since abandoned by the nice young woman who probably feared for her safety, not to mention questioned her future fertility options – and sit her down with my phone. I try to unbuckle her helmet strap and she smacks my hand away. Safety first during seated iPhone usage, apparently. I lean back and look toward the sky. What the hell is going on here? My children were *bleeding* for god's sake! I willfully let them try to injure each other? Child Protective Services would probably frown upon things like this.

With no phone to distract me, I watch Jack and Emmie from a distance. Jack has abandoned his helmet, but Emmie's is still firmly anchored to her head. *She looks ridiculous*, I think, *but if he pushes her again, at least she won't suffer a head injury*. Small victories.

Jack climbs up on top of the equipment, in a manner I'm sure was not intended when they built the structure, and I wait for the inevitable fall. But he maintains his balance and deftly swings down without incident. It's funny, when he was two years old, I would stand right behind him, holding his hand on the steps, boosting him up, catching him at the bottom of the slide. I couldn't fathom a time when I wouldn't hover and help. But slowly, he started doing it on his own. When did I stop worrying so much and let him do it on his own?

Duh, there's the answer to this whole thing. I can't helicopter them forever. I can't boost them up and then catch them, preventing them from making mistakes. Just like on the playground, they need to climb and fall and climb again. They need to learn to do it for themselves. Sure, there will be some skinned knees and tears. I can lift them up and boost them for the rest of their lives, but I can't prevent them from falling. I just have to hope they know how to right themselves when they do. And that I will always be there to hug the tears away.

Right now, in the midst of the parenting, it's hard to see the end result. But just like at one point, I couldn't see anything except the never-ending cycle of breastfeeding and diaper-changing and sleep charting, it's hard to see the time when I won't be responsible for their decisions, for their very well-being. It makes me think about a conversation I had with Emmie last week when, while making her a lunch based on a very specific set of her requests, I rhetorically asked her what she would do if I wasn't around to cater to her every need.

"I don't know Mommy, but Jack is the only one who knows how to use a knife," she said, licking almond butter from her fingers. "So he'd have to start making our food."

Someday, my kids won't view me as their everything. In a few short years, they'll actually view me as nothing they want anything to do with, especially in public. And I get that. But for now, I'm still the one making most of their choices for them. I shop for their clothes, prepare their food, check their homework and schedule their activities. But now I see I need to involve them more in the process. I need to ask what they actually want – as well as what they think. Because by doing *for* them all the time, I'm not teaching them *why* or *how* to do things. And more important, I'm not allowing them to experience the consequences of making their own choices.

And that's the reason I decided to embark on this journey in the first place. Less control for me and more control for them. Hopefully their control results in less bloodshed, but I don't have high hopes for the immediate future. I sigh, staring at the tree branches above me. Maeve giggles and shoves my phone in front of my face. Her favorite activity is looking at my photostream and she waves the phone at me, the picture a blur. I reach out to stabilize it and see what she's looking at.

"Look, Mommy! We are eating Chick-fil-A!" she says gleefully.

Maybe it's okay to still make *some* of their choices in the future. Like ones involving my personal political and social views as they relate to chicken establishments.

CHAPTER TWENTY-ONE
FACING YOUR FEARS

I can't believe it, but I made it thirty days. I am giddy with anticipation when I wake up this morning. This is it! One more day – a piece of cake. Although, this could definitely be the hardest day of the bunch as this is the day I'm actually revealing the project to the kids. Up until now, I wanted to keep it secret for a few reasons. One, I wanted to see if they would notice I was changing my parenting style. Two, I didn't want them asking for nonsense things just because they knew they could. I mean a trip to Six Flags was one thing, but a trip to Disney World is another. And third, I didn't want a trio of judges gloating every time I broke the rules, because I knew I would break the rules eventually.

I wander downstairs to find the Three Musketeers watching TV on the couch, lined up in birth order from left to right, all with his or her own blanket. American cheese wrappers litter the ground and a trail of granola-bar crumbs leads from the couch to the garbage can. I ignore the mess and tell them I have something to talk to them about.

"Have you noticed that Mommy hasn't been saying no lately?" I ask.

"Yes," Jack says suspiciously.

"Well, Mommy is doing something called Yes Mommy and today is the last day of my project," I say. "I've been doing this for the last month and today you get to do anything you ask."

"Why?" Emmie asks, probably suspecting some sort of catch. My children are notoriously suspect of unfamiliar situations.

"Well, I thought it might be fun."

"Can we have pancakes from Old McDonalds for bwekfist?" Maeve asks eagerly. My kids have always called it Old McDonalds and I never correct them because it's adorable.

"Yes!" I yell, raising my hands above my head.

"Can we eat them there?" Jack asks, again with suspicion.

"Yes!" I yell, again raising them above my head and doing a little jig.

"Can we have syrup?" Emmie asks excitedly, getting into the spirit of the morning.

"Yes!" I yell, turning in circles on the rug with my arms stretched into a V overhead.

All three kids jump up and down on the couch, which of course results in Jack jumping a little too roughly and knocking Emmie off the couch, onto the floor, which causes an onslaught of tears.

"Guys, let's take it easy," I say, pulling Emmie onto my lap and hugging her. "Now, we need to get dressed if we're going to start our big day. Anything you want, this is it. This is your chance."

We arrive at McDonald's and pile into a booth. Normally, the syrup is carefully calibrated at home – organic maple syrup from actual maple trees, none of that caramel-colored fake sugar crap that will make you grow a third arm – and doled out by me. But today, Jack pours three packets of the fake crap on his pancakes and asks for a spoon to get the excess off his Styrofoam platter. Mmmm, brown Styrofoam, the breakfast of champions. Maeve is happily slurping an orange juice and dipping a whole pancake into a puddle of syrup on her own Styrofoam tray. Emmie is taking bites of a breakfast sausage and telling me it's the best thing she's ever eaten. I really need to introduce her to foie gras.

Once they've digested the food and the full sugar rush takes hold, we head back to the car and head toward home down Clybourn Avenue, the Chicago skyline looming in the distance. "So, what do you want to do next?" I ask. I'm terrified of the answer, but pleasantly surprised when Jack yells, "Can we go to the top of the Willis Tower?" Yes, yes we can! I haven't been to the Willis observation deck since I was in college and the kids have never been, so we get to play tourist in our own town today. As we cross the river on Ashland Avenue, Emmie spies a boat and quickly asks, "Can we take the water taxi there?" Of course! We drop the car at home, cobble together a backpack with snacks and sunscreen and walk over to the water taxi dock, where we luck out to find it is leaving in two minutes. The kids are welcomed aboard by the captain and quickly scramble to the railing for the best views. Why haven't we ever done this before? It offers amazing views of the city with no traffic hassle. I want to get a job in the Loop just so I can take the water taxi every morning! Wait, no. Not even a daily water taxi could persuade me back to a cubicle.

We exit at the Ogilvie station and walk the short distance to the Willis Tower. As an aside, I still can't get used to calling it the Willis Tower – it's the Sears Tower in my mind and always will be. But the sign says Willis, so that's where we end up. We buy the tickets and wait patiently for the elevator to whisk us to the one-hundred-and-third floor while Jack reads aloud all the interesting facts about the tower. "Mommy, did you know the Willis Tower is two-hundred-and-eighty-two Michael Jordans tall?" he says. "Wait, who is Michael Jordan?" Oh dear god, my born-and-bred Chicago son doesn't know who Michael Jordan is? We have utterly failed as parents. We might as well put ketchup on his hot dogs and start referring to it as Chi-town.

"Well, he was the most famous and best basketball player in the world when he played for the Bulls," I explain.

"Oooooh, so he was like Derrick Rose," Jack says. Okay, we've done our part. He gets it.

"Yes, but without the injuries," I say. A man behind me in line snorts. I'll be here all week, folks! Tip your servers!

"Mommy, it says there are seven-hundred-and-ninety-six potties in this place!" Emmie cackles. She and Jack convulse in laughter. This is possibly the funniest thing they have ever heard.

"Potties? They have potties here?" Maeve asks seriously.

"They have potties everywhere, Maeve," I say. "Of course they have them here."

Maeve begins singing, "If you have to go potty, stop and go right away," to the amusement of the line snaking through the roped-off area. They can thank PBS and *Daniel Tiger's Neighborhood* for that very topical ditty. She stops suddenly and announces she actually has to go potty right now. Because of course she does. I ask her to please wait until we get to the top and she agrees to try. Fabulous. Jack has discovered the straps and poles used to create the line path separate and is gleefully unhooking a strap and letting it curl back inside itself over and over again. The next time he re-attaches it and readies to let it zip back again, I grab the strap with my hand and stop it. A security guard steps toward us and tells Jack to stop touching the straps. Jack looks at the rent-a-cop and touches the strap with his index finger. Oh my god. I hiss in his ear, "They will ask you to leave if you don't stop and trust me, the tallest building in America is not the place you want to challenge a security guard." Jack shrugs away from me and yells, "We're next!" as the elevator doors open. Saved by the bell.

The kids count along with the floor numbers on the ascent, which takes an astonishing sixty seconds. The doors open to reveal glass windows in every direction, sun streaming into the one-hundred-and-third-floor Sky Deck's air-conditioned hub. The kids immediately run to the first bank of windows, crossing the rope with a sign that says Please Stay Behind Rope and start yelling out landmarks. "I see Soldier Field! I see the White Sox Field! I see a train! I see the lake! Look at the little cars!"

We wander around to the lake side, oohing and ahhing over Navy Pier and the Ferris wheel. I point out that you can see both Michigan and

Indiana across the lake today and they are appropriately impressed. We wander around to the north and point out Wrigley Field and I show them the general vicinity of our house, using buildings close by as landmarks. "I see our house!" Maeve says. Really? Bionic vision on this one. We should get her signed up for baseball because the hand-eye coordination has got to be off the hook.

And as we move to the west side of the building, my kids stop dead in their tracks. Before them lies The Ledge. I totally forgot about the recent remodeling project at the Willis Tower, which added retractable glass cubes that extend four feet from the side of the building. Standing in the glass cube gives you a view straight down one-hundred-and-three floors to the street below. "Can we go in there?" Jack asks breathlessly. And before I can answer, he leaps into the cube and jumps up and down three times on the glass floor, eliciting stunned gasps from the adults in the vicinity. Clearly, a seven-year-old boy isn't going to bring down a structurally-engineered glass cube, but the irrational part of every adult brain screams "No!" when he or she sees it in action. I actually grabbed for him as he did it, and then realized how silly I was being. One woman gives me a dirty look and I mutter under my breath that people standing outside of glass cubes on the one-hundred-and-third floor shouldn't throw stones.

The three kids go out as far as they can, squealing about how cool it is. Jack lies face-down on the glass, arms and legs spread akimbo. I feel sick just watching him do it. I can't bring myself to step onto the glass floor. I'm not scared of heights, never have a problem flying or with roller coasters, but for some reason, the edge of things freaks the living hell out of me. When we go to Hawaii, I'm the ledge Nazi, making sure everyone stays well back and has secure footing. I'm not a huge fan of diving boards and don't get me started on the ridiculousness of bungee jumping. Maeve has her hands plastered to the outer edge of the cube, looking straight down at her feet and beyond, while Emmie bends her knees into a frog pose, hands on the floor in front of her, staring down at the street below.

"Mommy, come out here," Jack yells, "you have to see this!"

I am frozen to my spot on the floor outside the cube. I look down and my stomach turns. "No, Jackie, I'm fine."

"Mommy! You said no! You can't say no today!" Emmie sing-songs to me. Oh shit.

"Yeah, Mommy, you have to say yes. You said so!" Jack chimes in.

I take a deep breath and look straight out toward the horizon. I got this. I put my left flip-flop out on the glass floor and then my right. I don't want to look down, but it doesn't matter because my peripheral vision shows me the clear surfaces all around me and I can't help but look down. Oh dear god. I am standing one-hundred-and-three stories over Wacker Drive with nothing but a piece of glass suspending me there. I quickly step back, but smile at the kids. "See? Mommy did it!"

"Mommy, you should lie down like me," Jack says. Thanks for the option, but I got this, Jack. After snapping a few shots of the kids, they reluctantly leave the glass cube to complete the full circle of the tour.

"Mommy, why didn't you want to do that?" Jack asks. "That was so cool!"

"Well, you know how sometimes you are scared to do something and then Mommy and Daddy make you do it because we know you'll like it in the end? Mommy was scared to go out on the ledge but I did it anyway."

"Why didn't you like it?" he asks.

"It kind of made my tummy hurt," I answer truthfully. "But I did it anyway and I'm glad you made me."

I refrain from giving him the big speech about the Willis Tower Ledge being a metaphor for parenting, how moms and dads are scared to have kids, how they're scared that they're not doing the right thing, that they're not good enough or patient enough or strong enough, but that they swallow their fears and do it anyway. I also stop myself from telling him that Yes Mommy was all about testing limits, letting go and doing something that doesn't feel exactly right. Nor do I tell him that I'll never do it again.

We finally tear ourselves away from the view and head down to ground level, where the elevator dumps us out in the middle of a gift shop. Seriously. Chicago-themed gifts as far as the eye can see and not a "no" in sight. The kids beg for souvenirs, so I allow each of them to pick one thing. Jack chooses a small Chicago taxi replica, which is different from the other fifteen tiny cars and trucks he has at home in that it says Chicago on it. Emmie immediately grabs a Hello Kitty wearing a Chicago shirt, which is different from the other fifteen Hello Kitty stuffed animals she has at home in that it says Chicago on it. Maeve chooses a giant, round, rainbow sucker, much like the ones you see kids licking in movies. It does not say Chicago anywhere on it. This is different from, well, she doesn't have any of these suckers at home, so it's certainly different in that respect. The kids then spy a food court in the Willis lobby and ask to eat lunch at the Corner Bakery there. As I love me a Corner Bakery Rueben sandwich, I am more than happy to say yes. I am saddened to say yes to the soup, sandwich, chips, chocolate milk and cookie each child insists on ordering. And of course each child must have his and her own of each of these items.

Fifty-seven dollars later, we're seated at a table surrounded by office workers when Maeve drops her cookie and loses her mind. Hysterical tears, flailing arms and legs and screaming at decibels normally only heard by small dogs completes her ensemble for the show. I try valiantly to calm her down, but she's sobbing into my neck about the injustice of it all. Jack and Emmie eat their own cookies, savoring bite after bite, demonstrating the proper way to hold a cookie and take bites like they're filming a how-to video for YouTube, which infuriates Maeve even more. Suddenly, a woman appears at the table with a cookie in her hand. She's dressed comfortably in black pants and a red cardigan sweater, obviously used to the indoor climate of the tower.

"Would this help, sweetie?" she asks Maeve. Maeve solemnly nods her head and takes the cookie and thanks the woman without prompting. I thank her profusely, digging in my pocket for cash. She waves me off. "I'm a grandma," she says. "I know." She smiles at Maeve, compliments her dimples and gestures to the other two. "Savor it now, they'll be big before you know it."

Usually, I'm annoyed when people say this to me. It's usually at some inopportune moment, when the kids are throwing tantrums and I'm at my wit's end and I want nothing more than to snap, "I can't wait until they're big." But today I nod and smile. I really do need to remember this, the days where they think Mommy knows everything and can't stand to be away from me. The days where all we had to worry about was what time we'd get home for nap and what we'd have for snack. The days where Mommy said yes to the water taxi and the Willis Tower and conquered her fear of stepping outside her comfort zone.

CHAPTER TWENTY-TWO
NOW WHAT

It's done. I did it. Thirty days of yes. I'm alive, I have all my faculties about me, I haven't lost any limbs (although I did shed some blood) and I seem to have come out unscathed. But my kids are another story.

After settling in to the land of "normal" parenting once again, I find the re-entry is tougher than expected. Emmie, especially, doesn't know what to do with herself. After a month of essentially getting whatever she wanted whenever she wanted, she's now confronted with the stark reality that "no" is once again a part of my vocabulary.

"Mommy, can we have ice cream?" she asks one night. The day in question was filled with fighting, hair-pulling, attitude and a less-than-willing stance on doing chores. When I ask you three times at eight in the morning to make your bed, and it's still not done at four in the afternoon, I don't consider that complying. My patience was a nub of its usual self, which isn't saying a lot, and I calmly told her no, we would not be having ice cream for dessert because no one's behavior warranted it.

"What?" she screamed. "That's not fair! I want ice cream!" This scream was accompanied by a full-out tantrum, complete with kicking her feet and rolling around on the floor. I coolly stepped over her prostrate body, making my way into the kitchen, were I calmly poured myself a glass of sparkling water. Sipping the cold bubbles, I watched as she flung herself around, crying and whining about the unfairness of it all.

"I liked you better when you were Yes Mommy," she yells, snot dripping down her face, ponytail askew on the back of her head.

Didn't everyone?

Truth be told, this little experiment really has mellowed me as a mother. They say it takes three weeks to make something a habit, and that sounds about right to me. After that second week, I started to hit my stride and it became reflexive to say yes, rather than no. And while the month is officially over, I do find myself saying yes more than no.

But there are things I refuse to negotiate on. Candy is once again verboten. The first time Maeve sweetly asked for a bag of M&Ms and I refused, she looked like I had slapped her in the face. "But I want M&Ms," she said, repeating herself as if I misunderstood. I told her that no, we would not be having M&Ms for a morning snack and offered her a banana instead. Apparently, a banana was not to her liking, which I ascertained by her reaction, which was to spit on the ground at my feet. Guess who got a timeout instead of a banana?

Bedtimes have also returned to the "strict enforcement" category, which was met with some resistance by Allied Forces. The first few nights they waged a fierce campaign filled with multiple room-vacating strategies that employed tactics the best soldiers would be proud of. They stormed the hallway in pairs, hid in the bathroom closet during stealth reconnaissance missions, army-crawled their way out of bed and consulted maps for the best routes to and from the border without encountering government forces. The rebels fought a tough battle, but the parental troops were able to contain them by outwitting them and threatening economic sanctions.

But I'm also more apt to let things slide. You want to wear a Little Mermaid nightgown as a dress along with your Minnie Mouse sunglasses paired with an armful of bracelets, Hello Kitty tattoos up and down your arms and your Uggs in the middle of August? Knock yourself out. You want to wear this ensemble to Trader Joe's and push the little cart? Be my guest.

Jack recently asked if he could skip his nightly shower so he could finish the last few chapters of his *Magic Treehouse* book. He didn't need to ask twice. A well-read child can always shower the next day, and the passion for reading shouldn't be denied. He'd been in the pool that day anyway, so that kind of counts as showering, am I right?

We've gone to the park more, ridden bikes more and, strangely, gotten along more. When I was in the confines of the "yes" stricture, I felt so much pressure. I literally couldn't say no, which heightened every interaction with my kids. I was constantly self-editing, self-correcting and self-conscious. I spent large portions of my day either worrying what outlandish thing the kids would ask for or fretting that something I had just said yes to was going to ruin our lives. And once the month was behind us, and I was no longer contractually obligated to say yes to everything, I realized I was saying yes on my own terms, which was really satisfying.

Emmie had the hardest transition, but Jack might have benefitted the most from the experiment. As the first-born, he's obviously our experimental child. We figure it out with him, refine it with Emmie and perfect it with Maeve. Or just give up caring about the issue with Maeve. Case in point: the fireplace. When Jack was little, we were total freaks about not touching the fireplace in the living room. Never mind that we have not used said fireplace since he was born, we were determined that he know the fireplace was off-limits. And oh, how that fireplace played its siren song for him. Redirection, stern warnings, timeouts, nothing kept that child from touching the fireplace except the passage of time and the expansion of his world. When Emmie was old enough to move, we once again started the fireplace shuffle, this time barricading it and making it inaccessible to inquiring hands. She was still curious, but redirection worked like a charm. By the time Maeve was mobile, we literally could not have cared less if she touched the fireplace. I found her inside the fireplace once and instead of sending her to timeout, I took a picture and laughed. Third kids have it easy.

But this experiment leveled the playing field. I was saying yes to Jack just like I was saying yes to Emmie and to Maeve. And he couldn't have been happier. But he also showed me that the parenting we've done up to this point had an impact on him. He made good choices even when confronted with the ability to go crazy, and when he did make questionable choices, he knew it.

Maeve was still too little for this to really make a difference. She was happy to go along with the program, enjoying the ice cream and the late bedtimes and the unlimited screen time. But she won't remember this and it probably won't have a lasting impact on her.

I think the lasting impact is the growth we've had as a family. The kids won't look back in twenty years and think about that one day I took away the iPad because they didn't clean up the toys in the basement, but they might remember the time we went out for ice cream and doughnuts after bedtime. They won't recall the morning Mom screamed so loud she lost her voice (I hope), but they'll remember the time I let them all have a sleepover in Maeve's room. They won't remember me insisting they eat their broccoli, but they damn well better remember the time I took them to Six Flags on the spur of the moment. I want my kids to remember me as a fun mom, the mom who laughed, the mom who cared more about loving them than punishing them. I don't need to be their best friend. Kids need structure and guidance and rules and consequences and I know that. But it's not going to ruin anyone's psyche to have a mom who occasionally throws caution to the wind and "okays" a spontaneous mental-health day off school.

Going into this experiment, I was terrified. And the reaction of every single person I told about my plan was equally as terrifying. But I had nothing to fear. Let's be honest, my kids are not sociopaths. They don't play with matches, they don't hurt animals, they don't (seriously) injure each other. Well, not very often. But my parenting playbook was full of reasons why they *couldn't* do things, not reasons they *could* do things. And most of those things I said no to weren't a big deal.

Yesterday, we were walking to the park when Jack picked up a rather large rock near the curb. I opened my mouth to say no and gulped instead. I waited to see what he planned to do with this rock before I passed judgment. Emmie and Maeve were pretending a neighbor's stone retaining wall was a balance beam, which is also normally forbidden, and I was equally as cavalier with them. If they fell the twelve inches to the ground, it was their own faults. Jack tossed the rock from hand to hand a few times before raising it back like a baseball. I started the "n" sound with my mouth when he brought it down to his side without any intervention. As we got a few paces ahead of him, he gently dropped it near the curb and ran to catch up. Emmie and Maeve gracefully stepped down from the rock balance beam without incident and twirled their way up the sidewalk. The three of them walked ahead of me and I realized standing there that we had come full circle in that exact spot from where it all began. A stick, a rock, one boy, two girls and lots of impulsivity. The first time, my reaction set a chain of events into motion that included an injury, a punishment and the idea for a crazy project. This time, my non-reaction resulted in a non-event, just another walk to the park. Nobody yelled, nobody got hurt and nobody conceptualized a new literary tome because there was no need. I like to think it was a combination of lessons learned and natural consequences enacted. In reality, it was probably a combination of those things – along with luck – that Jack didn't throw the rock, hitting one of the girls, sending her to the emergency room for stitches and sending me into a tizzy of lectures and disappointment.

And in my long and illustrious parenting career, I have found that almost everything can be attributed to luck. Luck in conceiving, luck in birthing a healthy baby, luck in bringing the baby home and not dropping it, luck in making it through the first year, and the next and the next. The dirty little secret among parents is that nobody really knows what she or he is doing when it comes to raising kids. Oh sure, some might act like experts, but they're just throwing stuff at the wall and hoping it sticks – just like the rest of us. Attachment-parenting, sleep-training, potty-training, free-range parenting: it's all the same, do what you think is best for your child and your family and hope it doesn't produce a serial killer. And if you do, by chance, produce a serial killer, society will blame your parenting anyway, so you really can't win.

In the end, I think that month did make a difference. I'm more laid-back, more willing to bargain and more willing to laugh when Maeve takes her clothes off on the sidewalk outside of Uncle Julio's Hacienda rather than freak out and forbid her from having dessert. I mean if she wants to walk home without a shirt on in protest of some perceived toddler injustice, am I supposed to quash her very own March On Washington, err, March on Chicago? If Emmie wants to watch the last fifteen minutes of some princess movie before bath time, does it really cause the earth to spin off its axis? If Jack plays another life on *Temple Run*, will it *actually* rot his brain? Of course the answer to all those things is no.

Or rather, the answer is yes. Yes to more fun, yes to more laughter and yes to chilling the hell out and enjoying life with kids. Except when one of the girls comes to me and asks for a tramp stamp – then the answer is a resounding no.

ACKNOWLEDGMENTS

To my agent, Jessica Faust, thanks for the encouragement and the early revisions. To my editor, Stephanie Elliot, your eagle eye, grasp of language and grammar rules and input to the manuscript were immensely helpful. Forget this Arizona thing and move back to Chicago already, would ya?! And to cover designer extraordinaire, Dar Albert, you've done it again!

To my book club girls, after eleven years, we're still going strong. Thanks for the thoughtful discussions about both books *and* pop culture. There's less wine but more substance these days.

To Leah, Nancy and Samantha, thanks for listening to me blather about my writing (among other things) at our monthly dinners. New books, new jobs, new houses, new babies and we still make time for each other.

To Ally, Jen and Vicki, if I'd just known about the magic elixir that is the BBC during this crazy month, it would have been a whole different story. Thanks for your witty commentary and convincing me no one will die if my kids stay up past nine o'clock. Joanne, Heather, Leah, Mandy and Maureen, thanks for inadvertently taking part in the process.

To Heidi and Ian, long live The Biking Feinermans! Can't imagine dinners and lunches without you. Well, without Ian. We have lunch without you, Heidi, all the time. But only at three-week-old Asian spots featuring the chef of a chef.

To my Mexican Fiesta celebrants, (Jen, Evan, Vicki, Mark, Ally, Chris, Ed, Niki, Beth, Kevin, Nancy, Marnie and Rundio) we'll always have Grandma.

To my parents, Mary and Dave, thanks for the never-ending material. Also for your encouragement and enthusiasm for everything I do. To Beth and Kevin, I'm serving scrambled eggs at every meal from now on. Thanks, as always, for participating in my nonsense projects and adding some great material.

To my in-laws, Marilee and Scott, thanks for your support and interest in all my ideas, as crazy as they might be. To Marnie, I still don't think you actually moved based on the amount of time you spend here. Thanks for always pimping me out on Facebook and supporting the cause.

To Josh, your willingness to live our life publicly and let me document it is one of my favorite things about you. That and your constant reminders that it's good to be Amy Sprenger. Thanks for your help, your not-so-subtle suggestions, your sense of humor and your looooooove. Also, your intense feelings about Canada.

To Jack, Emmie and Maeve, may the ensuing years be filled with lots of yeses. Well, within reason. Without the three of you, our lives are less crazy, less fun, less rewarding and less expensive. I am so lucky to be your mom. Now please, put your shoes on. Shoes! Now! Please! I said, *put your shoes on*!!

ABOUT THE AUTHOR

Amy Sprenger is an author and award-winning blogger at SnarkyMommy.com, where she tells it like it is and isn't afraid to make fun of herself or her questionable parenting prowess. A former news and sports reporter, she lives with her husband and three children in Chicago's Lincoln Park neighborhood where she silently judges all the other parents.

Other Amy Sprenger Books

Baby Bumps: The Almost, Barely, Not Quite True Story of Surviving Pregnancy, Bed Rest and One Batshit Crazy Family

Over My Dead Potty

Facebook: The Snarky Mommy
Twitter : @SnarkyMommy

www.ingramcontent.com/pod-product-compliance
Lightning Source LLC
LaVergne TN
LVHW051126080426
835510LV00018B/2254